... Every Purse and Purpose

General Motors and the Automotive Business

Also by John W. Wysner

Anatomy of A System

Rays of Hope

About the Author

Author John Wysner has worked closely with the top executives in the American automobile industry for the past twenty-nine years. He served as a principal consultant to General Motors Corporate Staff and vehicle marketing divisions on a number of standards-based management, business planning, and customer satisfaction systems. He designed and managed Chevrolet's in-dealership Service training, and set up management systems for GMC Truck, GM of Canada, Oldsmobile, and Chevrolet.

John Wysner is the President of The High Performance Group, Inc., a Southfield, Michigan firm. He is a member of the American Management Association, American Society for Training and Development, Society for Technical Communications, and is a winner of several National Awards for Service Training for General Motors. He is the author of *Rays of Hope* and *Anatomy of a System*, books on the Auto Industry. He is a Gold Leaf Contributor to National 4-H Council, one of the country's largest youth development organizations, and a Strategic Planning Consultant to 4-H. John Wysner is listed in Marquis' *Who's Who* and in the U.S. Registry's *Leading American Executives*. He is pictured above with his grandson, Aidan.

... Every Purse and Purpose

General Motors and the Automotive Business

John W. Wysner

© **1994 by John Wysner and General Motors**

Wilderness Adventure Books
P.O. Box 217
Davisburg, Michigan 48350

Wysner, John.
    --Every purse and purpose : General Motors and the automotive business / John Wysner.
        p. cm.
    Includes bibliographical references and index.
    ISBN 0-923568-39-5
    1. General Motors Corporation. 2. Automobile industry and trade--United States--History.   I. Title

HD9710.U54G499 1994   338.4'76292'0973
                                                            QBI94-732

Manufactured in the United States of America

Contents

Acknowledgement

. . . *Every Purse and Purpose* is the culmination of the author's 30 years working in and for the American automotive industry. Its purpose is simple; to use the full range of knowledge acquired working in every facet of this fascinating business to provide perspective for newcomers to the business and (hopefully) insight for its managers as they lead it into its second century.

I owe thanks to a great many people in the business for the opportunity to work and learn in virtually every function in the automotive arena. But particular thanks are in order to John Rock of Oldsmobile and Jon Harbaugh of GMC Truck who have done so much to help make this book possible.

It is my sincere hope that . . . *Every Purse and Purpose* will return something to a business I feel is, without doubt, the most pivotal economic and social "definer" in world commerce. In particular I hope it will be a useful tool in the reengineering process that General Motors is undertaking to solidify its historical position as the world's premier automaker.

John Wysner
Detroit, Michigan

Prologue

On completion of his master reorganization plan for General Motors in 1926, GM President Alfred P. Sloan was asked if he could capture in a sentence or phrase the essence of the redesigned automaker. "Certainly," he said. "General Motors will provide a car for every purse and purpose." In that simple description was embodied the most powerful marketing and manufacturing strategy in the history of the automotive business, a strategy that would make GM not just the premier automotive manufacturer, but in time, the world's largest company.

In the 70 years since Mr. Sloan coined his description of the, then, "New General Motors," the auto business and the world have changed dramatically. It's been said that "the more things change, the more they stay the same." As the auto industry enters 1994, and its third (depending on how you count) global reengineering, we'll see that the old saw is probably more true than ever. As GM changes its structure and strategy, it may in fact find itself returning to its roots, which came to be called the "cradle-to-grave" strategy in the 1930s.

As this generation's "new GM" emerges, we may well find it reestablishing the unique brand imagery that aligned each of its divisions with a different segment of the economy and social strata. But this time, the alignment will extend beyond the cars and trucks and their prices to include the "bundle" of customer services that further signifies what each GM division stands for. This development is a direct function of the new-found, absolute importance of the customer—the most changed component in the automobile industry. This idea—the focus on the customer and GM's (and the industry's) response to achieving this focus is what this book is all about.

The American automotive business reached its hundredth anniversary in 1993. It has been, in so many ways, the most interesting and important century in the history of world technological, sociological and economic development. The automobile, more than any single invention, changed the world from an agrarian to an industrial society. The automotive business was born and grew around the mass production factory, a development that revolutionized the manufacturing process for **all** industries. Perhaps more significantly, it became the most important single factor in the shift from a rural to an urban society, and in the growth of the infrastructure, the evolution of the middle class, and the multicultural integration of American society.

Mass production and the changes it brought to our lives and economy is the phenomenon normally thought of in connection with the automobile industry. But there is another area just as profoundly impacted by the automobile—the advancement in the structure of business and marketing that the car business has brought. Just as Henry Ford is credited with being the father of the mass production factory and the fully integrated modern industrial complex, GM's Alfred P. Sloan must be credited with being the father of the modern "command-control" vertical business concept with its centralized administration and decentralized operations functions, and of much of modern marketing science. Sloan's design of the early 1920s, GM's first reengineering, was as radical and important an advancement in the science of business and marketing as Ford's assembly line process was to manufacturing technology. In combination, these two men and the generations of designers, engineers, marketers, and business executives they fostered, would make many of the most profound contributions ever to societal change.

The automobile business grew rapidly from a hand-built, cottage industry to be the source of the world's largest and most profitable companies. And in the process, it became the country's major employer and one of the most important factors in the global economy. It hasn't been an easy evolution, but it has always been a fascinating one.

For nearly 80 years, the auto business represented the ultimate manufacturer-driven, steady growth industry. Then, after the paradigm shifts in world politics, consumerism, conservation and environmentalism that all came together in the early 1970s, the car business—and virtually **all** business—changed rapidly to a market-driven, intensely competitive global gameboard with a whole new set of "rules" and priorities. In the past 15 years, it has become a business working desperately to shift to an external, customer focus; moving rapidly from setting its own priorities to reading and responding to the priorities of its customers. This dramatic change has brought about the third major reengineering of General Motors, and of **all** the major players in the auto business, in the past 75 years.

Without question, this 1990s reengineering will be the most significant in automotive history. It will do far more than position the domestic "Big Three" of GM, Ford and Chrysler for continued growth and profit. It will, in all likelihood, be the key factor in deciding the world's economic "winner" in the developing contest between the massive free-trade markets represented by NAFTA, the European Economic Community, and the possible foundation of an Asian consortium. In this process, the core strategy originally devised by Sloan's GM in the 1920s—"a car for every purse and purpose," a marketing concept we've come to know as cradle-to-grave, is re-emerging in a far broader context as the key to this global economic battle.

This book will attempt to tell this story. Its goal is to be both a past and "future history" of the automotive business. Its focus is, of course, General Motors—the world's largest, most influential and important automaker. Its hope is to serve as an informational tool in GM's recreation of itself as the most successful of the world's new breed of "manufacturer-service" industries.

Introduction

The Auto Industry in Twentieth Century Economic and Social History

The twentieth century has seen the most fascinating growth and interaction of industrialism and social evolution in modern history. In a span of less than 50 years, the United States became the world's dominant force in both military and economic influence. And during this period, the country's three major domestic automakers grew from non-existence to become the world's largest businesses, most prolific employers, most powerful drivers of related industry, and the industry's most profitable organizations—all within less than 25 years!

Oil clearly replaced coal as the single resource most vital to global commerce and as the pivot point in world political and military focus, largely due to the automobile and truck. In a span of only a dozen years, from 1903 to 1914, the automotive industry advanced from a hand-built, "cottage industry" to the basis for the mass production factory that would be, arguably, the single most powerful change force in technological and social development since the foundations of the industrial age in the railroads and factory-machinery of the mid-nineteenth century.

The automobile, and the industrial and infrastructure that quickly sprang up around it, also spawned many of the innovations in modern

5

business and management science. In fact, no single area of human endeavor has had a more pervasive impact on the business, economic and social history of this century than the evolution of the automotive business. Automobiles and the infrastructure necessary to create and support them—commercial, financial, societal, roads and highways, businesses and industry supporting and supported by the car and truck, housing and urban construction, etc.—have reshaped our world and changed our lives more profoundly than any other industrial, social, or scientific development in modern history. Let's take a look at some of the more important impacts the automobile has had on our lives and lifestyles . . .

- It changed America and the world from an agrarian to an industrial-based society in two decades.

- It replaced railroads and waterways as the primary arteries of commerce. And, it quickly became the favored form of personal transportation, replacing the mass transit of the time.

- It was the transition industry from the "Coal Economy" of the nineteenth to the "Oil Economy" of the twentieth century.

- It was the birthplace of the mass production factory and the societal restructuring that followed it; as Henry Ford said, "the organization of man, machines, and materials into one, productive whole."

- It changed the core focus of industrialization from the product to the process, through constant manufacturing technology improvement to make the product more stable, useful, and less expensive to produce.

- It revolutionized the manufacturing process and turned cottage industries into multi-billion dollar, complex corporations.

- It created the affluent middle class, and in the process, totally reshaped the distribution of wealth. For the first time in history, the laborer became the principal customer for his products.

- It changed and defined the marketing process into a powerful form of major communication and social influence, and in the process, reshaped mass-media advertising.

- It contributed a global supplier superstructure that rapidly became the world's biggest employment network.

- It was **the** key factor first, in the movement of mass population to the cities, and then, in the redistribution of these populations to the "suburbs"—purely a phenomenon of a mobile, affluent society.

- It evolved "Fordism"—markets, customers, Dealers were all part of the "social mass production-consumption" system.

- It focused on the **process**—to make the product more saleable, profitable, useful—as the principal job of business.

- It drove the growth of the infrastructure that "shrunk" our geography, and created an integrated economy, and finally a truly global network of commerce.

- It forged a common link between business-social-political evolution.

- It shaped economic and political development and patterns of social and commercial legislation more powerfully than any other industry.

- It evolved the concept of "market segmentation" and the idea of graduated enhancement of products as a means of differentiating social class and complete lifestyle definition.

- It became a prime mover of cultural evolution, impacting art, film making, entertainment and music in ways ranging far beyond the industry.

- It became the core of a systematic attempt to solve the social and political problems, as well as the economic and environmental evolution, of an industrial civilization.

- It deeply affected social status in diverse areas such as work, leisure, housing and lifestyles by making mobility easy, affordable, and a "social statement."

- It was a key factor in the growth of labor unions to a position of equality with management and ownership, and the redistribution of wealth that evolved with the labor movement.

- It helped to define social responsibility through particularly powerful impacts in consumerism, environmental stewardship, and safety.

- It played a key role in the evolution of government intervention in both business and personal lives through fuel conservation, pollution control, safety legislation and the powerful and permanent bureaucracies fostered by government's growth to support the expanding regulatory role.

- It brought about the development and evolution of the modern corporation. It enabled the decentralized, multi-divisional structure of industry that began with GM in the late 1920s, that replaced the nineteenth century holding-company design that characterized "big business" before Alfred Sloan.

- It defined organizational structures and management techniques more than any other industry, particularly Sloan's many innovations at General Motors.

- It evolved the concept that franchise owners needed to be profitable if the manufacturers were to succeed, and were key image and customer good-will resources for the manufacturer.

- It virtually invented marketing and production strategy—GM's cradle-to-grave process, i.e., "every purse and purpose," that helped restore much of the American economy and helped to bring the country out of the Great Depression of the 1930s.

- It evolved the concepts of "disposable" products, used-products markets, and installment buying that shaped so much of the socio-economic evolution of this century.

- It brought about, more than any industry, the business-government partnership that was to shape economic development and wartime strategy.

- It shaped modern marketing, particularly in the use of advertising and the electronic mass-media. In the 1950s, the "annual announcement" became an American institution, contributing to the creation of "pyramid segmentation" in Sloan's GM.

- It had a unique impact on world politics and politicians: Ford's "Peace Ship" in World War I and his relationship with Woodrow Wilson, A.P. Sloan's close ties to Franklin D. Roosevelt and their impact on the Depression and World War II, Ferdinand Porsche's ties to Adolf Hitler and building the German armed forces in the 1930s. All were pivotal in shaping the economic-industrial-military complex that led to World War II and the "new post-war world." Truman and Henry Ford, Sloan and Eisenhower, Reagan and Iacocca continued the unique, powerful auto-political relationship over the past four decades.

- It was the key to war production and weapons technology. The industry's aircraft, ships, engines, tank, trucks, personnel carriers, weapons, and electronics production, perhaps more than any single factor, led to allied victory in World War II.

- It has been, more than any other industry, the key to world commerce and global economic rebuilding after four wars. In the process, the industry was the key driver in making the U.S. the world's foremost military power and commercial leader.

- It has become the largest direct/indirect employer in global industry (responsible for one of six jobs), and has the greatest positive impact on the unparalleled standard of American life.

- It has had the single greatest impact on shaping the franchise business through the evolution of the automotive Dealer, and on much of state and federal regulation of commerce in this century.

- It has been largely responsible for the uniquely American evolution of entrepreneurship that has marked its own growth and that of its suppliers.

- It is a key factor in the development and growth of many other industries: Travel, Transportation, Commerce, Sports, Insurance, Utilities, Postal Services, Interstate Commerce, Highway Construction, Consumerism, Film Making/Entertainment, Commodities—farming, mining, steel, electronics and computers, and many others.

- It evolved the concept of market segmentation—the linking of customer requirements to socio-economic application of products in terms of roles they play in social status, as well as utility and commerce.

- It linked business, government, finance-economy and commerce more than any industry.

- It was at the heart of America's rise to export-trade leadership during the 1950s and 1960s, and helped make the U.S. the free-world "spokesman" and international business leader, and with electronics, was the key to Japan's rise in the past thirty years.

- It has had a greater impact on a broader spectrum of technology than any other industry, notably in powertrains, electronics, computers, sound systems, pollution-control systems of all types, steel, plastics, adhesives, military, commercial transportation, communications, battery technology, and a host of others.

- It became the source of power in the highly influential highway lobby, resulting in the development of the infrastructure that marked the geographic expansion of industry and the population.

- Because of its commercial, technological, economic and social impact, it played a key role in the success of free-market capitalism and the failure of totalitarian government in Europe and Asia.

- It has played a principal role in the depletion of oil reserves, and in the process has been a principal shaper of the "Politics of Oil."

- It has been a principal driver in the growth of the middle class world-wide, and its impact on world commerce.

- Its products have become "personalized" for applications ranging far beyond basic transportation to lifestyle/status statements.

- It largely shaped the evolution of financing and credit buying.

- It has become the prime mover of the American Economy in this century.

- It evolved as a principal generator of state and federal revenues from vehicle and gas taxes.

- It has grown until, today, all business and commerce is high-way-related; interstate trucking carries the mainstream of commerce; over 80% of **all** commerce is motor-vehicle dependent.

- It created the single element, the motor vehicle, most respons-ible for a uniquely American way of doing business—from advertising to franchising to shopping to retail trade—a concept that has spread world-wide.

- It has been a focal point in development of the three world free-trade markets, the realignment of political boundaries, and redefinition of world economic power around the three powerful trade blocks: EEC, NAFTA, and the potential Asian Consortium.

- It has been, with the computer industry, a driving force in the business reengineering process that is reshaping the structure and strategy of world business in the 1990s, as was done in Sloan's "Command/Control" GM design of the 1920s.

- And finally, the culture and economic strategies of nations have become embodied in their automotive industries and in the "personalities" of their largest automakers.

The automobile, more than ever in the 1990s, is becoming the key element in shaping the economic evolution of the next century. The battle between General Motors, Toyota, and Volkswagen—as the economic "point guards" for their countries and the free-trade markets they represent—will likely spell out which culture, lifestyle, values set, and economic philosophy will dominate world trade in the 21st century.

The purpose of this book is to examine this amazing phenomenon called the automobile, and its far-reaching impact on business, culture, economics, and social development. We'll review the first hundred years of "the business," decade-by-decade. And then we will analyze the interactive impact the auto business has had on the economy, and on the development of two equally fascinating trends—the automotive Dealer as the world's most complex franchise business, and the empowerment of the customer in the paradigm shift from a manufacturing-driven to a market-driven business economy. This history will form a foundation for understanding the "change events" that brought about the reengineering of the company and the industry in the 1990s. Finally, we will look ahead and try to get a handle on what the next century might hold for us all.

The Expanding Importance of the Customer and Customer Services

One of the most important functions in the automotive company of the 1990s is customer services. In the intensely competitive car and truck marketplace, the customer has clearly been empowered as the "key market driver," and customer satisfaction has long ceased being a "nice to do" activity. Superior customer service, resulting in satisfied, loyal customers, has become the most important competitive differentiator in the automobile industry. In fact, merely satisfying the customer in the 1990s is no longer enough. The winning automaker in this decade will be the one who **consistently delights** the customer throughout the complete ownership life cycle, from first awareness to vehicle repurchase.

All the major automakers, domestic and foreign, are well aware of this. A manufacturer's customer satisfaction rating in the industry has become its most coveted goal, replacing things like "car or truck of the year" awards that recognize strictly product excellence. In fact, product quality, long the most discussed marketing concern, has been relegated to an entry-level qualifier, something a manufacturer must have just to go to market. The great pay-off of the 1990s is, without question, the customer. The company that best understands the requirements of the customer, is the most responsive to these requirements, and provides the best overall treatment, and learns to do it **proactively**, will emerge as the ultimate winner.

The scope of customer satisfaction in the auto business has also taken on a new meaning. Once relegated to the Service Department/fixed operation of the Dealer and manufacturer, satisfying the customer now spans the full ownership experience from first awareness, to shopping, to buying, delivery, warranty service, customer-pay service, and the repurchase decision. Every department in every automaker's marketing division, manufacturing group, engineering department, and parts organization now shares equal responsibility for understanding, satisfying, and "delighting" the customer. Strategies to ensure the convenience and satisfaction of the customer have achieved parity alongside new product development and manufacturing/distribution technologies with the industry's senior managers. What was once a public relations, service-based issue has now reached the status of a top priority survival strategy with every manufacturer's Board of Directors.

One of the obvious results of this situation has been the emergence of manufacturer-based customer and Dealer contact processes. And the contact process has expanded and intensified through the use of 800-lines and interactive databases supplementing live contacts at auto dealerships. As the expense of maintaining a large in-field wholesale staff has become prohibitive (especially in GM, which still has the industry's highest cost-per-unit vehicle expenses), the reliance on centralized contact using computer systems and "communications highway" technology has become a must.

With this movement, several important things have evolved:

1. The customer assistance and Dealer Sales/Service Manager functions have become **strategically pivotal** in customer service, more so than ever before.

2. With this importance, the **empowerment** to satisfy customers and Dealers focused in these positions has increased.

3. At the same time, since the results of the activity directly impact every automaker's income and profit, customer satisfaction, and owner loyalty, the **responsibility** focused on the customer and Dealer contact positions is greater than ever before. At a given moment, a large number of people, relatively new to the business, will be making more decisions that will have more direct bearing on saving (or losing) customers and satisfying (or angering) Dealers than will any senior executive of a car company's home office.

To carry out this contact and decision-making process consistently and confidently, in a highly successful manner, the company's customer and Dealer contact people must understand and apply knowledge in many areas, some obvious and others not so obvious. Let's take a look.

- They should have a strong grounding in **how the industry works and its history**. The automotive business is a unique and fascinating story, and the more the customer-Dealer contact people understand about how it has come to work the way it does, the better the quality of their decisions.

- They must understand **how a manufacturer works**; how they spend and make money. And they should know the strengths and weaknesses of their manufacturer relative to their competitors. And, of course, they must understand the business interactions process between their company, its Dealers, and their customers.

- They should be **current on all of their products**—operating characteristics, problem areas, and status on changes and fixes.

- They should understand **the fundamentals of the economy**, the drivers of economic cycles and the impact of these cycles on the business, and on each of the players—manufacturer, Dealer, and customer.

- They must understand that **unique business person, the Dealer**. What the traits of a successful Dealer are. What is required to build a successful retail business. What the Dealer's motivations, needs, and expectations are. How they make (and lose) money. And they should, ultimately, be able to analyze an operating statement and understand the strengths, weaknesses, and opportunities of the Dealer involved.

- And of course, they must understand and **have a level of real empathy with the customer**—their requirements, their expectations, their frustrations and confusion. And they must form teams and networks with their counterparts in the automaker's technical assistance, field service, and engineering areas to bring all the necessary resources to bear on quick, fair problem resolution.

The result of this knowledge will help the contact person do one of the most difficult things in the business—balance expense management and customer satisfaction so that the end result is profit today and retained business for tomorrow.

To really be good at this balancing act, there are three important tools. The first is **knowledge**—a thorough understanding of the players and the things that impact the business. The second, and one which is tougher to measure, is an **entrepreneurial spirit**. Another phrase that describes this is "ownership mentality." The more that the manufacturer's contact people "feel" their work and the decisions they make affect the success of the business, and the more personally they take the performance of their company in the business, the better they'll do their job. After all, those Dealers are selling and servicing "your" cars and trucks. Those customers are dependent on the manufacturer's representative to make "their" company work for them. The company is counting on its contact people to spend its resources wisely, protect and support its Dealers, and retain its customers. And "the company's" shareholders are looking to protect the value of their investment and its high returns. Really feeling that these things are true, and maintaining an absolute commitment to win requires the spirit of personal ownership, and the knowledge that what the wholesale contact does impacts the company as much as the actions of any employe possibly could.

The third tool at the wholesale contact's disposal is **teamwork**—working with their District counterparts in technical, warranty management, Dealer operations and customer relations. The great advantages of teamwork are advocacy and experience/expertise. By integrating functions, backgrounds and knowledge, there's a much greater chance of reaching a balanced decision—one that is best for the customer and the company. And perhaps the most important aspect of teamwork is learning to reach consensus, the point at which each point of view is heard and integrated into the team's decision.

The Spirit of Entrepreneurship

One of the most dramatic changes in the automotive business in the last 90 years is the importance of customer and Dealer telephone contact. This job has evolved into a position requiring an entrepreneurial spirit. It is a product of the massive cost-cutting since 1989, which has taken many experienced managers out of in-field contact jobs and replaced them with telephone contact people in home offices. The primary reason that the replacements had to be made, despite the need to cut costs, is the ever increasing importance of understanding and responding to customer requirements, and helping the Dealers to also improve their customer skills.

For a number of reasons, mostly focused on the competitive value of quick, high quality customer response, these positions have evolved rapidly to be highly empowered and highly influential. The type of person most successful in this role will have many traits. Perhaps the most important is an **entrepreneurial spirit**. Here's why this is true:

The Contact Person in an automobile company, to be successful, must adopt a **truly** entrepreneurial attitude—a real "ownership mentality." They are continually making decisions that commit the resources of their company. Being a front-line influencer of both their customers and product distributors (Dealers) makes this a must. The automaker's customer/Dealer contact person, perhaps more than any other employe, "wears the hat" of the company and division. They must be constantly aware of this responsibility and represent their organization with the same attitude and commitment they would if they were its president or chairman.

More than **any** business owner, the automotive customer contacts deal with customers on **three** levels—the end-users of their products (customers), distributors of their products (Dealers), and designers and builders of their products (manufacturers). The variety of internal and external "customers" dealt with by the telephone and field contacts is certainly one of the broadest in the industry.

The first requirement of a successful automotive Customer Relations and Service Manager is to have a highly-developed knowledge of their products, their company's policy and programs, their distributors' operations, concerns, and problems, and the needs and expectations of their products buyers. They should, ideally, be the best informed people in the organization in all of these areas. And where change and complexity make it impossible to "know everything," they must have immediate access to information and expertise.

Because of the wide span of knowledge required, the manufacturer's contacts must maintain a total view of the business. First, they must have a short-term focus on the immediate needs of their company to stay in business and make a profit, and the immediate needs of the customer and Dealer to solve current-state problems. But they must also have a long-term view of what it takes for their company to grow and prosper. This involves thinking about "desired-state" strategic issues like building owner loyalty, their role in building market-share, and what is required to build the financial health of the Dealer Network and manufacturer.

To accomplish these short/long-term goals, the customer-Dealer contact person must have, in addition to a strong knowledge base, good information gathering and problem-solving skills. Their problem-solving and decision-making ability must comprehend the importance of making decisions based on both a knowledge of each situation they deal with and the requirements of all the players involved—the customer, the Dealer, GM and the contact's marketing division. Consistency, balance, fairness, and empathy are all important characteristics for the successful customer and Dealer contact person.

Every operating function in a business that is based on systems will have process measures (to measure process efficiency) and business objectives (to measure effectiveness). The automotive customer contact person of the 1990s must be able to differentiate between process measures and business objectives, and know how to set priorities that satisfy both accordingly. They must maintain a top commitment to the customer-focused business objectives regardless of day-to-day process variance. (That is, they must work toward satisfying customers while managing their company's finances at the same time.)

The contact person must also develop a level of **consistency** in how they do their work. An exceptional, consistent performance is one that balances the requirements of all players, customer, Dealer, and company, is fair and logical, and works toward both short-term profit and long-term business development goals.

To do all these things, the automotive contact person must have a wide variety of knowledge and skills. They must understand company priorities and business policy. They must listen and "hear" customer requirements. They need to know the fundamentals of Dealer operations, business management, customer satisfaction, product operation and technical understanding, and state-of-the-art customer service strategies. And of course, they must have excellent interpersonal and communications skills supported by problem-solving and negotiation skills.

The customer/Dealer contact must always have the outlook of an entrepreneur—act as though they are aware that they are responsible for "signing their own paycheck"—for the ultimate success or failure of their company. Again, having the empowerment to spend resources and to influence customers and Dealers makes this a reality.

They must have an intense **empathy** for the business. As we'll see, the automotive business is truly unique. The contact person must have a feel for the problems that every manufacturer (most importantly GM) is facing today, and for the role they play in solving these problems. One absolute imperative of customer satisfaction excellence today requires the customer contact to have a deeper sensitivity and in-depth understanding of the automotive needs of the customer than ever before.

Finally, where the customer/Dealer contact could once focus on the relatively narrow span of their job, basically bordered by the "do's" and "don'ts" of a policy manual, now they must think of a much bigger playing field. They must understand that GM is not yet competitive in productivity and cost management; that GM's loss of market-share to a below 35% level threatens the complete fixed-cost infrastructure of the company; that the lowered value of GM's debt makes them less competitive in financing; that GM's product development cycles are too long and too far behind much of the competition; that they are too vertically integrated and costly; that their Dealer network is poorly placed and balanced; that there are still far too many product models; that much of the company still competes with itself rather than with the real competitors; that the value of the GM franchise has declined in the past five years; and that as yet, some of the company's executive management doesn't "practice what it preaches" about the customer.

At the same time, General Motors has many positives on the "plus" side of their business ledger today. Some important examples:

- Saturn's redefinition of product **and** process in GM and the **real** business importance of customer enthusiasm that they have demonstrated have helped to reshape GM's attitude and commitment to reengineer their processes and culture.

- The North American Automotive Operations (NAAO) Strategy Board has become a much more responsive strategy making process than the old management committees format.

- The company has reduced its models count, and is in the process of reducing the number of vehicle platforms it supports.

- GM has streamlined its decision-making process, and, as a result, its responsiveness to the market.

- The company's engines and "underskin" electronics/technology are exceptional and in many cases, industry benchmarks.

- The new North American Purchasing initiative pro improve the whole supplier relationships process

- The focus on common business processe promises to greatly improve efficiency and

- There is a new focus on retail, and the importance of helping to increase value-added and lower the cost-to-retail a unit and improve profit potential for a Dealer.

- There is a central position for customer focus in the evolving GM Vision.

- Structural and cost "downsizing" and stress on supporting GM's core business is refocusing the company on creating real value for the customer.

Given today's GM business scenario, General Motors employes have more say and probably the greatest opportunity in the company's history to have an impact and make a real difference in the company's future success. In the balance of this text, we'll investigate all these areas—the history of the business, the Dealer, the customer, the manufacturer, and the economy. We'll see how and why they affect one another, and how the business works with and for each player.

Section I. Development of the American Automotive Industry

Dynamics of the First 95 Years

This section presents the history of the American automotive business decade by decade from 1890 through the present. It focuses on the "business" history of the industry more than its products. The purpose is to give a sense of why and how GM and the business developed as they did.

Let's start by looking at a quick "thumbnail sketch" of the non-technical history of the car and truck business. This introduction will touch on some of the more important highlights in the industry's growth, in order to understand the more detailed analysis that follows.

1903-1920s

From 1903 until the late 1920s the fledgling automotive industry found itself in a "Friendly Incubation" period. It was a growing industry in an environment that was very supportive—socially, economically and from a competitive-marketing position. During this period:

- There was no serious foreign competition strong enough to vie with Ford and General Motors for market-share or force the direction of product or manufacturing standards. Products, performance levels, the service environment, and every aspect of the business was firmly in the hands of the emerging American manufacturers, particularly Ford Motor Company and a young General Motors.

- A relatively stable economy, except for the post World War I recession of 1919, favored business growth. And the transportation-based auto industry led the way as the country moved from a rural to an industrial society. Motor transportation opened up whole new opportunities for manufacturing, shipment of raw materials and components, and movement of finished products and workers previously at the mercy of waterways and railroad lines. This, in turn, drove the development of the national infrastructure and of many related businesses.

- Gasoline power was the clear winner over steam and electric engines. Oil's ready availability at low cost kept the customer base broad and growing and made motor vehicle transportation the most economical choice, fueling the growth of virtually every industry.

- Relatively slow technological evolution lowered manufacturing cost and extended tooling life and workforce skills. Early focus was heavily on the mass production factory and manufacturing technology, driven by Henry Ford.

- Mass production assembly with its lower costs, interchangeable parts, stable high output, consistent quality, and efficient use of resources was perfect for the new industry. And the size and growth rate of the young industry was so great that it brought with it a whole new middle class able to purchase the products and services they produced.

- Little or no unionization prior to the late 1930s further served to keep costs down.

- The cost of training was nominal due to longer equipment life, simpler product service, and the mass production factory process which greatly simplified the contribution of each worker toward the finished product.

- Because of these conditions—low competition, rapid growth, a supportive environment, and the "newness" of the business—automakers were largely able to "dictate" customer taste. The young auto industry was in a "manufacturer-driven" position in which the automakers could establish the requirements for products and performance.

- Annual cosmetic changes in cars and trucks made for low cost vs. high selling price, due to extended tooling life and high perceived value.

- The size of an automaker's market was basically equal to its production/distribution capacity, since the available marketplace, personal-use and commercial, was in a state of constant growth and expansion.

- From 1900 to the early 1920s, the industry was driven by manufacturing technology and price. A single product that was well-made, inexpensive and easily serviced (i.e., the Ford Model-T) was really all that was required to meet the needs of the "mass" market.

- In the mid-1920s, Alfred Sloan and General Motors made a dramatic change in this scenario with the advent of modern marketing and a range of products designed to meet different needs of different socio-economic classes of buyers.

1930-1970

From 1930 until 1970 the auto industry maintained success and profitability in a dramatically changing world.

- Domestic automakers still enjoyed many of the advantages of the first two decades of the business.

- During the Depression of the 1930s, GM's "cradle-to-grave" strategy and Alfred Sloan's reorganization gave the company the growth surge that first pushed it past the Ford Motor Company.

- The stimulation of wartime industry, in the 1941-1945 period, requiring accelerated production, tooling, technology, and resource applications from automakers, served to support much of the manufacturing growth needed for the post-war markets. New production methods, new product designs, and even new business organization and strategies would grow out of the demands of World War II.

- The mid-1930s brought the advent of powerful labor unions. While the unions did much to improve the wages, living standards, and benefits of the workers, raising the overall living standard of the American middle-class, the labor contracts also became a source of product cost that would haunt the industry with the later introduction of foreign competition.

- Post-war America of the late 1940s was the de facto world leader in every industry, and was the principal driving force in the world economy. A country hungry for new products (there were no new car models between 1941 and 1945) with a returning peace-time workforce was ready for the period of the industry's greatest growth and the country's greatest prosperity.

- During this period, the vertical "command-control" organization with centralized administration and decentralized operations, as conceived by Alfred Sloan, reached a high level of refinement. Most support functions were integrated into the company. Administration, Finance, Research, Marketing, and Policy were centralized. Line management, Sales and Service Operations were decentralized. Parts, manufacturing, and support functions were vertical. And there were separate brand business units—the company's marketing divisions—each with its own unique brand image and servicing unique market segments with its products.

- And the American auto industry was still benefiting from a "manufacturer-driven" non-competitive market dynamic. From the late 1940s and throughout the 1950s, the Industry found itself in a golden age of growth and development with few of the complex problems that awaited it in the late 1960s. Low taxes, inflation, and interest stimulated consumer purchase and industry investment and growth. Rapidly expanding suburbs and two-income/two-car families fueled economic expansion across virtually all industries that supported or were supported by the powerful Big Three of GM, Ford, and Chrysler.

1970 Until Today

There has been a dramatic shift to a "market-driven" automotive industry in recent years. This started with a "trickle" of interesting little foreign vehicles from the VW Beetle of the 1950s to the Japanese products in the early seventies that became a tidal wave of high quality Japanese, German, and other foreign vehicles, owning a third of the domestic market by the late eighties. The flood gates for competition were opened by the OPEC Oil Crises of 1973 and 1979, and fueled by rapidly growing government regulation, consumerism, and environmentalism.

- American industry simply did not respond to the shift to smaller, fuel-efficient cars driven by the oil crises of the 1970s. And industry didn't read the new priorities in quality, economy, safety, and customer services that these changes drove.

- There were volatile financial market changes as well, driven by expanding debt, deficit, taxation and inflation, resulting in an interdependent global economy.

- Auto financing and the **total** cost-of-ownership have become major marketing factors—driven by double-digit inflation in the late seventies and fueled by escalating costs of doing business.

- Fuel became a precious, expensive commodity with world political overtones—the "Politics of Oil."

- Technology of manufacturing and on-board product has been advancing at a "revolutionary" pace, with computers driving all vehicle systems, and robotics and other manufacturing innovation bringing dramatic change to the assembly plants.

- Continual government regulation—in safety and fuel economy requirements—has produced costly price increases.

- Growth of powerful labor unions, affecting economic and living standards, has driven the cost-to-compete even higher. GM, more than any manufacturer, has raised the living standards and benefits of the autoworker, and in the process, absorbed the industry's highest labor and benefitsrelated cost-per-unit.

- Costs of training and diagnostic equipment have become major Dealer expenses, making qualified technicians a precious resource in continual shortage.

- Parts costs and availability have become critical concerns.

- "Voice of the Customer" has become the key competitive concern.

- It has become continually more difficult for the manufacturer to realize profit under the increasing cost-to-compete, and the costs added by regulation, consumerism and 50 years of pattern-labor contracts.

- Market-share is no longer a function of manufacturing/distribution networks. Instead, worldwide over-capacity has made these areas a cost burden.

- Competitive pressure has been increased by knowledgeable, powerful consumer interest groups, which have further empowered the customer and made litigation and its spin-offs; (mediation and arbitration), a way of life.

Alfred Sloan's Impact

General Motors' business contribution to this history was overwhelmingly shaped by one man. In 1920, Pierre Dupont and J.P. Morgan, two of the most prominent "captains of industry" in the first quarter of the century, wrested control of a failing General Motors from William C. Durant. Under Durant, GM was a massive holding company (like most major industry of the period) that grew by acquisition—buying and selling independent companies. Under the new leadership, a man named Alfred P. Sloan became the president of GM, and was given the job of devising an all new organizational structure for the company. Sloan's design featured:

- Decentralized line management/operations.

- Centralized administrative, financial, marketing, and research groups.

- Separate manufacturing and parts operations.

- Dividing the product badges into separate business units, or Divisions.

- Separate Sales and Service operations, by Division.

- A personnel management function.

- A budget-driven focus for decision-making.

- A distinction between policy and operations.

- And a whole new way of doing business, driven by marketing science, and featuring cradle-to-grave strategies, annual model changes, financing of purchases and a new importance for the Dealer.

During Sloan's tenure, spanning five decades, not only would he make GM the world automotive leader, he would also develop and implement a business strategy that no less a management authority than Theodore Drucker would use as the prime example of management operational excellence.

The company that Alfred Sloan evolved was based on a unique and powerful strategy—the "cradle-to-grave" concept in which every age, social, and economic level of customer had a "logical home" in GM. This gave GM a market span unequaled by any other manufacturer, before or since. And it gave GM the leadership role in an industry that had been ruled by Ford Motor Company in its first quarter century.

This chapter examines Sloan's strategies, the industry they evolved in, and the new industry they shaped. And it looks at the last 20 years, the period of market-driven change. We'll see how the new priorities have changed the automotive business and what it all means for the future.

The chart on the following pages provides a "one-page reference" of major events in GM's Business History from 1890 to 1993.

A Timeline of GM Business History

Agrarian Society	Ford Founded	$5.00 Day	
Holding Companies	Durant Begins GM	Employe as Customer	
Assemblers, Not Producers	Olds, Leland;	Ford Grows on Profits	
	Mass Production		
1890	**1903**	**1911**	**1914**

Ford Model-T; Inexpensive Car for the Masses	Ford Highland Park; Mass Production Factory Ford Lowers Model-T Price Each Year

———————— Focus on Production/Price ————————

GM Redesign Complete	Dealer Network	"Cradle-to-Grave"
Central Administration (Command)	Operating Report	Segmentation
Decentral Operations (Control)	ROI Focus	Advertising
Modern Prototype	Brand Image	
ROI 80%	Growth, Demand.	Depression
	Undercapacity	1/3 Work Force Unemployed
		GNP at $80 Billion
1926		**1929**

Supplier Industry Growth	Low Fuel Costs	Ford Caught in
	Prosperity and Growth	Model Shift

Production/Distribution Capacity ▬ Market Share

———————— Age of Marketing/Business Begins ————————

Wartime Conversion of Industry "Suspends" Business Cycles	Pent-Up Demand Prosperity Begins; GI Bill, Employment "Explosion," Middle Class Grows	Government Support; Low Taxes No "Consumerism;" Social Issues	Plants/Dealers Expand Income Growth Ford goes Public
1942	**1945**	**1950**	**1956** **1960**

Technology Advances through Military Research	Suburbs, Multi-Car Families; Interstates	Annual Styling Change "Big," Soft Rides, Fast, Low Mileage,	Deming, Juran Bring Quality to Japan
No New Models		"Disposable"	

———— Return to Prosperity ————   ———— Golden Age of Exce

1890-1993

Birth of Vertical Manufacturing
Early Dealerships
Low Taxation, Low Inflation
Growing Wages

Commercial Growth/Post WWI
Infrastructure Development
Recession

Sloan Assumes Command
Marketing Focus Begins

1918	1920	1925

Industrial Growth
Urbal Development
Middle Class Evolves
Ford/GM Solidify Industry

Fuel Inexpensive
(Gas "Wins")
Continuous Growth

Rouge Complex
GM Business Reengineering

——————— Manufacturing-Driven ———————

GM
Product Reinvestment
Commercial Market
"Class-Mass"
Efficient Production
Dealers Focus
New Deal (FDR)
GNP at $40 Billion

Production Capacity,
Dealer Network
Expanded Rapidly

GM Takes Lead
From Ford

Emphasis on Short-Term Profit

WWII

1932	1934	1937	1941

Economy "Halved"
in 3 Years

Labor Unions Growth

Technology of Product a "Differentiator"

——————— Industry Redefined in "New Society" ———————

GM Share to 60%
Advertising

Priorities Shift
> Quality
> Economy
> Price
> Safety

Ford, Chrysler Refocus
on Product, People,
Engineering, Customer

Board "Revolt"
Reengineering Begins

Toyota "Crown"

Japanese
"Halo"

1972	1983	1992	1993

Oil Crises
High Taxes, Inflation
Social Consciousness
Consumersim
Government Rgulation
Costs Passed to Customers

Reorganization of GM
> Automation Focus
> Loss of Core Marketing Strategy
> Poor Quality
> Product Strategy Fails
> High-Cost Producer
> Japanese Share Climbs

——————— Shift to Customer-Driven ———————

The Phenomenon of the "Car Business"

To further understand the development of the automotive industry, let's examine the factors that have made the car "business" unique. The balance of this book will develop understanding of this business in detail. Here are some of the most important features to watch for.

- Historically, the production and distribution capacity of auto and truck manufacturers dictated their market-share. This was true since, for much of the industry's history, there has been a growth market "protected" from the outside and fueled by positive economic, government, and social growth and support.

- The market was constantly expanding over the first 85 years; there was little or no foreign competition for the first 70 years of the business. So domestic manufacturers who were capitalized to compete could control much of their own destiny. Ford, General Motors, and Chrysler became the world's largest and most profitable employers.

- However, the automotive business has become intensely competitive over the past 20 years, with strong foreign intervention and a number of factors that shifted control to customers.

- This intense competition, with early, strong leads by the Japanese, has forced U.S. manufacturers into an uphill battle regarding quality, customer satisfaction, image, productivity, and cost management.

- One of the things that the automotive "Business" requires, for a company to be successful, is a **perfect balance** between well managed warranty (product quality, cost-per-unit, and serviceability) and customer satisfaction (services and experiences that create a positive relationship between factory, Dealer, and the customer over every aspect of the ownership cycle and customer experience). This situation involves one of the most complex educational challenges in American Industry, that of convincing both vehicle manufacturers and Dealers of the long-term business value of customer satisfaction. Customer satisfaction has long been measured and marketed, but only recently has the recognition evolved to an understanding that business success, market-share, and profit will be directly affected by the manufacturer's ability to understand and respond to the **customer's** requirements better and faster than the competition.

- In the past, many Dealers relied on their factory wholesale contact to act as a "claims clerk." A great amount of manufacturer's time and manpower was spent correcting and deciding the validity of Dealer warranty claims.

- In like manner, Dealers have often been reluctant to pay adequate salaries for quality warranty management people and a Customer Assistance Manager (in larger dealerships) to be the customer's advocate across departments.

- So, in the past, the customer has often been caught in the give and take between Dealer and Factory, with the result that no one wanted to take responsibility for a problem, leaving customers unhappy and frustrated.

- A properly managed warranty can be one of the best customer satisfaction tools, since it means quality repairs, Dealer profit, more flexibility in policy, and owner retention. When customers get what is rightfully due them, in the form of a correct first-time repair, everyone involved prospers. Warranty is **not** a remedy for poor training or a way to "balance the ledger" with the manufacturer. This type of thinking has caused many of the problems with less successful Dealers.

- The Auto Industry has always been a "point-guard" industry for the national and world economy—due to the massive workforce directly and indirectly employed by the industry, and to the role of motor vehicles in driving world industrialization and the growth of commerce.

- Multi-brand badges in one dealership (a practice called dualing) and population growth have caused many metro Dealers' sales volumes to outstrip their ability to service the greater numbers of customers. A good Dealer will always balance the ability to sell volume with an ability to properly service that volume, and a good manufacturer will demand they do so.

- Database technology has made tools like the various Dealer, vehicle, customer history databases and Warranty Management System possible. Getting Dealers to understand and use them is one of the next great challenges. A good Dealer can accurately predict customer satisfaction trends by tracking vehicle and customer histories through these databases.

The keys to dealership revenue flow, in **all** economic times, are the Service and Parts Departments, called the fixed operations. The business done by these departments, both warranty and customer pay service, can pay all the business' fixed expenses and even provide overall profit in tough times. An efficient, productive Service Department pays operating expenses, and can even carry Dealer profit in economic downturns when customers can't afford new vehicles and when maintenance and repair of their current cars and trucks is most important to cost-conscious customers.

Traditionally, a point of tension and distrust between factory and Dealer has been reflected in warranty, because Dealers feel the factory sends mixed signals (tight control of cost in recessions/satisfy customers during prosperity) and the Dealers want full self-authorization. Manufacturers apply continuous pressure for customer satisfaction, but in tough economic times, often clamp down on warranty expense. The right answer is sound warranty management, top quality products, highly trained technicians, proper parts inventories, and customer convenience systems—all **in balance**.

With the expense of automotive vehicles today, the marketplace feels that either warranty or policy should cover all situations—basically, customers want "lifetime warranties"—so the Dealer often becomes the customers "advocate."

- Some Dealers will often use warranty to make up for poorly trained technicians who don't diagnose and repair problems the first time. This is an educational problem requiring that these Dealers understand the long-term business implications of not satisfying customers.

- Dealers who feel "wronged" by the manufacturer often try to "balance the ledger" through warranty charges and policy requests. Again, better communication and education are required. Dealers must understand that any action they take that punishes customers and increases an adversarial position with the manufacturer can only harm their business in the long run.

- Product failure trends that customers don't want to pay for are often assumed to be warranty problems, even for vehicles far exceeding time and mileage guidelines. Keeping on top of field situations, providing good field fixes, and speedier manufacturing changes are required here.

- Great pressure is thus brought to bear on the people deciding on warranty and policy requests.

- Dealers will often play "you guys fight it out," telling the customer that "only the factory can decide on that." There must be true empowerment and a willingness by both manufacturer and Dealer to put the customer first.

- Therefore, Dealers' "service-ability" has become either a principal competitive advantage or weakness. Those who have the ability and commitment to meet the customer's needs and expectations consistently and without "hassle" have a huge competitive advantage in the customer-driven marketplace of the 1990s.

- Again, the answer to all of these situations requires:
  — Top quality products
  — Well trained Dealers and Technicians
  — A responsive parts organization
  — Competitive warranty systems
  — Cutting edge information management systems
  — Customer-focus
  — New types of companies that are truly "learning organizations" whose vision is based on customer empathy
  — First-hand knowledge of vehicle and customer histories
  — A top technical assistance organization,

And most of all

  — A knowledge of the requirements of customers and a strategy to consistently meet them.

This introduction has provided a brief summary of the conditions that shaped the auto industry and the priorities for success that have evolved between 1980 and 1990. The rest of this section will examine the business first century in great detail, to provide an in-depth understanding of the industry's growth and clues for its future success.

Chapter 1

The Birth of the Industry (1890-1914)

A Nineteenth Century Environment

At the dawn of the American automotive industry, the United States was still an agrarian society. Farming was the backbone of commerce and the great majority of the country's population still lived on working farms. Business was defined by two extreme structures. Big business was (the oil and railroad companies are the most notable examples) primarily organized as holding companies. In this design, a central management group ran a very diverse affiliation of companies, each of which tended to produce their own products, do their own hiring and firing, keep their own books, and set their priorities quite independent of the organization's other holdings. Acquisitions and liquidations were common and happened without any real regard for a "master plan" for the business. At the turn of the century business structures were either cottage-industries—the many small companies that dotted the landscape of American cities—or holding companies—with one management for a loosely connected group of businesses.

In either design, manufacturing businesses were primarily "assemblers," and not producers of final products. They bought parts and assemblies from other small manufacturing companies, and assembled the product they were selling. This structure was the approach followed by most of the early automakers, most of whom got their start in the horse-drawn buggy/carriage industry.

Some of these early automakers who were to become major pioneers in the business were Ransom E. Olds, William C. Durant, Max Grabowsky and Henry Leland. William Crapo Durant was the owner of the Durant-Dort Carriage Company in Flint, Michigan. "Billy" Durant was typical of the late nineteenth century deal-makers whose interests were in finance and in buying and selling companies to build ever-larger organizations. But, as we'll see shortly, Durant differed from many of his contemporaries in that he was a true visionary. He saw the automobile as the principal trend and dominant industry in the new century.

Ransom Eli Olds was basically an engineer. Unlike Durant, Olds was fascinated by the mechanical aspects of the automobile. With his partner Henry Leland, Olds would become the first pioneer of true mass production from his automobile assembly plant in Lansing, Michigan. The Olds Lansing facility was the first automobile assembly factory to mass-produce gasoline-engine-powered "horseless carriages."

When the Olds Plant burned in 1901, only one automobile was saved, a little runabout prototype that was to become the famous "curve-dash" Oldsmobile. Olds and Leland rebuilt and began production of the curve-dash Oldsmobile in 1902. This famous automobile became the first mass-produced, mass-marketed/low-priced motor car. In building the curve-dash, Olds used a basic assembly line process in which the product moved along from one assembly station to the next. And Olds was the first to use interchangeable parts. The Olds Lansing Plant produced 12,500 curve-dash Oldsmobiles by 1904. The curve-dash Oldsmobile was the first truly practical mass production gas-powered vehicle, capable of 40 miles per gallon and a road speed of 20 miles per hour.

The team of Ransom Olds and Henry Leland would establish a standard of excellence and quality that would be a hallmark of General Motors for the next 75 years. Leland, who split off to form Cadillac Motor Company, traveled to England in 1909 to enter the first Dewar Competition. In the competition, Leland's team completely disassembled three Cadillacs, mixed the parts thoroughly, and then reassembled the cars from the mixed pile of parts, components and assemblies. The reassembled motor cars were then driven 500 miles with no breakdowns or failures. As a result, Leland and Cadillac were awarded the coveted Dewar Trophy as the "quality standard of the world." Cadillac would win the award again for Charles Kettering's self-starter, probably the most important single invention in terms of making the automobile completely practical transportation for **everyone**.

A third major component of the early General Motors that took place in the first decade of the twentieth century was the pioneering of commercial trucking. Max Grabowsky and his family built and sold the first commercial truck in 1900.

He went on to organize Rapid Motor Vehicle in 1902, incorporating it under Grabowsky Motor Company, or GMC (the famous acronym that so many mistake for General Motors Corporation). William Durant would consolidate Rapid and Reliable Motor Company as a component of General Motors in 1911 to form the GM Truck Company.

Durant incorporated General Motors in 1908, bringing together Olds, Buick, Cadillac and GM Truck Company. He then took the company public in 1911. William Durant's stated goal was to build an automotive industry. His vision was to build a wide range of products for what he was sure would become a broad market with many levels of transportation needs—a major divergence in philosophy from his contemporary and principal competitor, Henry Ford of Dearborn, Michigan.

The early General Motors of the 1903 to 1920 period was noted by Theodore Drucker in his landmark 1953 text, *The Concept of the Corporation* as "a loose federation of independent chiefs."

The young GM's cast of characters included:

- William C. Durant—the founder and visionary leader who would be an early pioneer in marketing theory.

- Ransom E. Olds—the founder of Oldsmobile Motor Company and the first mass production automobiles.

- David D. Buick—the founder of Buick Motor Company, the original foundation of GM.

- Henry Leland—Ransom Olds' partner who would found Cadillac and become known as the builder of the highest quality cars in the young industry.

- Charles Kettering—a pioneer inventor who developed the self-starter and manufactured other firsts for Cadillac and General Motors.

- Walter P. Chrysler—GM's first great manager, who would run Buick Division and become responsible for much of GM's business success between 1910 and 1920, and who would go on to found Chrysler Corporation.

- Charles W. Nash—also an early head of Buick and President of General Motors, who would also go on to develop a major American motor car company.

- Louis Chevrolet—a famous designer and racer of the 1900 to 1920 period who, with Durant, would found Chevrolet Motor Company which would become the volume producer to directly challenge Henry Ford's Model-T for industry leadership.

Other contemporaries of Durant's would also make their mark as important pioneers in the early auto industry. People like Frank and Charles Duryea, makers of the first commercial automobile (1886) and the Dodge Brothers, early contract manufacturers for GM and Ford Motor Company, who would go on to found their own independent automobile company that would ultimately become part of Walter Chrysler's Chrysler Corporation. But none would have a greater impact on the automobile business, and on the social and economic history of the century than Henry Ford.

Henry Ford was born on a farm in what is now Dearborn, Michigan in 1863. A young man of little formal education, he had great natural mechanical and engineering genius. Ford would found the Ford Motor Company in 1903 and would originate the world's first, true **mass-production factory**. Ford's dream was to build an inexpensive car for the masses that would be totally reliable and easily maintained. Henry Ford would establish the Ford Motor Company as the clear industry leader in manufacturing technology, low-price, and market-volume and market-share in the industry's first twenty years.

Birth of Mass Production

Ford's philosophy went far beyond the new automotive industry, and would have a profound impact on society and the world economy for the major part of the twentieth century. Everything Henry Ford did was based on the premise that the functions of society and commerce were agriculture (to "grow"), manufacturing (to "produce"), and transportation (to "carry") goods. He believed that any enterprise, to be for the betterment of society, had to incorporate an interaction of these three functions. He further felt that the mass production process was the linkage between these functions, and that the production process should be built around the best product. Throughout his career, Ford would focus on the production process over the product itself, and on the belief that the true goal of manufacturing was to refine the production process to build the product faster, cheaper, better, and with less waste than any competitor.

In a 1926 book, Henry Ford defined mass production as, "the organization of man, machines and materials into one productive whole." His vision, therefore, extended far beyond the world of manufacturing automobiles to encompass a set of values for society based on work and production as the basic human virtues.

Theodore Drucker, one of the finest minds in business management and economic strategy, noted that Henry Ford made the "only systematic attempt to solve the social and political problems that came with an industrial civilization." The Ford philosophy, followed religiously throughout his long, industrious career, was to:

- Raise wages continually
- Cut prices continually

- Produce volume, quality products, and

- Increase profits continually.

According to this philosophy, Ford defined the first two decades of the business, through the early 1920s, as the "manufacturing era" of the automotive business, a period characterized by mass production technology to build cars and trucks in high volume and at low price. The two most important indicators of Henry Ford's philosophy centered around his beliefs about prices and wages. He lowered the price on his famous Model-T Ford every year between its introduction in 1908 until its final year of 1926, an 18-year span that saw 15 million Model-Ts produced! During this time, in 1914, Henry Ford made his most famous innovation. At a time when skilled craftsman were making from a $1.00 to $1.25 per day, Ford raised the average wage of basic Ford Motor Company assembly plant workers to $5 a day!

Detroit immediately found itself flooded with laborers from the northeast and farm workers from the south wanting to be part of the amazing Ford Motor Company. Politicians, economists, bankers, and business leaders almost universally criticized Ford's move as one that would cause "chaos and collapse" in the national economy. It did not. What it did was revolutionize the economy—creating a whole newly affluent middle class, demonstrating the great profitability of Ford Motor Company, and providing the first true recognition of the worker as customer. Until the $5 day, laborers typically built products for an upper economic class who did not make their money working as laborers in factories. With the Ford move, the size of the automotive market rapidly expanded. He realized his dream of "transportation for the masses" and solidified the conversion from nineteenth century agricultural to twentieth century industrial society.

Changing Business in a Changing World

While Ford was rapidly evolving and bringing low-cost mass-production to the young automotive business, Durant and Louis Chevrolet were also busy bringing about change in Ford's one real competitor, General Motors. Here's the sequence of events that would define the first of several major organizational restructurings in GM.

- First, Durant lost control of GM to the banking interests when he overextended the company financially in 1910.

- Rebounding very quickly, Durant formed the Little Motor Car Company in 1911.

- Next, he combined with Louis Chevrolet to join the Chevrolet and Little Motor interests to form Chevrolet Motors in 1912.

- Together, Durant and Chevrolet began large volume production of Chevrolet cars at multiple production facilities across the country. The "490" Chevrolet became the first serious competitor to the Model-T at comparable price, quality, and volume in 1914. With this product, Durant had what GM did not, a mass-market, low-cost, high-profit automobile.

- As a result, Durant was able to use the more valuable Chevrolet stock, in a five-to-one trade, to regain control of General Motors in 1918.

Ford was **not** a proponent of marketing or advertising. As a matter of fact, he was very opposed to marketing strategy as being wasteful of important resources better spent (he felt) on production facilities and technology. Henry Ford's basic approach was to ignore the actions of competition since he firmly believed that the best, cheapest products would market themselves, and that the best advertising strategy was to have the most reliable and inexpensive cars readily available in the greatest numbers. In all ways, he was a pragmatist and a "mechanic," and not a businessman or marketer.

As a matter of fact, the dominance of manufacturing over marketing was common across the young auto industry between 1900 and 1915. Remember, it was basically an industry run by financiers (like Dupont, Durant, and J.P. Morgan) and engineers (like Leland, Chrysler, Nash and Ford), and not by professional business managers and marketers. It was clearly a period of price and capacity competition, a rapidly growing young industry in which manufacturers were defining markets and products—one of the purest examples of the manufacturing-driven market in which demand outpaced supply, and the producers could dictate product and price acceptable levels.

The world of the automobile Dealers of this period was very different from today's. In the early Ford Motor Company, distribution of product was rigidly controlled by the factory. The Dealer was not really considered to be a key part of the system. Instead, like marketing and advertising, they were more of a "necessary evil." Factory-managed large Ford stores distributed products through secondary, privately owned outlets. Policy was **very** strict; sales quotas were absolute requirements, and overall, the seeds of the adversarial relationship that would come to characterize the later factory-retail relations, were sown.

In 1915, Henry Ford's $5 Day had become a reality. Durant was poised to reenter GM on the huge success of Chevrolet. The mass production factory was a great success with Ford's highly successful new Highland Park Plant. The automobile—a curious novelty only a decade before—was now selling nearly four million units a year. With these accomplishments, the automobile business had created a demand and a buying population far beyond Henry Ford's dreams of 1903. The young industry was poised to reach its next plateau, a shift in focus to marketing and management innovation.

Chapter 2

Marketing and Management (1915-1925)

America Shifts to an Industrial Society

The American automobile business, as typified by Ford Motor Company in 1915, was a highly vertical, integrated manufacturer. Most of the process, from raw materials to finished products, was controlled directly by the manufacturer. The mass production process had evolved to the point where semi- and unskilled labor controlled most assembly plant jobs. The integration of the factory led to a number of changes in business and society, most notably:

- The industrialization of society
- The growth of cities around manufacturing plants
- The rapid expansion of the national infrastructure
- The growth of the automotive supplier industry
- The concept of worker as customer and evolution of the middle class
- The growth, with the huge influx of unskilled workers, of early management-labor friction.

Another important feature of this period was the rapid evolution of the business to the point that there was no **real** competition for Ford and GM. It was a world of two very well capitalized, high volume/

low cost mass producers **vs.** a large number of small volume, more expensive niche products that didn't really compete for market-share with the "Big Two."

In this environment, as noted earlier, the automaker could dictate product levels, service levels, and price, typical of a developing manufacturing-driven business. In the decade between 1915 and 1925, both manufacturing and product technologies evolved rapidly. The impact of mass production and precision, interchangeable parts was felt across **all** U.S. industry. As the automobile and the infrastructure supporting it developed, America rapidly became mobile. Patterns of employment, leisure, trade, and housing developed around the automobile. Ford and GM rapidly became the nation's (and the world's) largest, most profitable employers.

Gasoline remained readily available and inexpensive. It was **not** a design limiter. This factor, as much as any, shaped the first 70 years of the business. In the process, the oil age of the twentieth century replaced the coal age of the nineteenth. The automobile replaced the railroad and shipping as the principal form of business and leisure transportation. And the United States replaced Great Britain as the world's top commercial power.

Ford During the 1915-1925 Period

In Ford Motor Company's second decade, Henry Ford solidified and retained central control of his empire; no problem was too large or too small to escape his attention. As part of Ford's plan for the growth of the company, it was important that the control of all resources, production and distribution remain within the company—and under Henry Ford's supervision. So, he began a process of full vertical integration (Ford ownership and management) of the complete manufacturing process, from raw materials mining, to rail and ship transportation of materials to the foundry, to parts manufacturing, to assembly, to product distribution through servicing. Highland Park Assembly Plant and the Rouge Complex became fully self-contained industries. The Rouge Complex was a virtual closed city with shipping docks, railroad terminals, aircraft landing strips, foundries, assembly and shipping facilities. By 1927, employment at "the Rouge" exceeded 50,000 and the complex became known as the "Cathedral of Industry."

Ford even maintained close control over his employes' personal lives. The vast majority of Ford workers lived in company-owned housing. Ford's "Sociology Department" kept careful track of the activities of all Ford employes, regularly calling on their homes to make sure that husbands brought paychecks directly home, didn't drink or smoke, were attentive parents, and in all areas lived moral, healthy lives (as defined by Henry Ford). This intense involvement in workers' personal lives became a principal factor driving the early labor movement.

And during the company's second decade, Ford continued his obsessive focus on manufacturing and price, always looking for greater efficiency and a cheaper product. Little or no attention was paid to marketing or to new product development—the Model-T, a car for the masses, remained the company's total focus—a situation that would soon hurt Ford deeply.

GM During the 1915-1925 Period

While Ford continued focus on one car for the masses, with top focus on the manufacturing process, Durant at GM was thinking along a very different line—different products for different price ranges to serve a broader segment of the market, and to provide a hedge against economic slumps. Alfred Sloan, in the second half of the 1920s, would refine and make this idea GM's core strategy for the next 60 years.

It was also during this period that GM would embrace marketing, design the modern corporation and perfect the business concepts that would serve all of the manufacturing economy well into the 1980s.

The principal differences between GM's strategy and Ford's during the industry's second decade can be summarized:

- While Ford continued to focus totally on manufacturing process, GM became a principal driver in defining modern marketing.

- While Ford continued to produce an inexpensive single product in high volume (the "mass" theory), GM under Alfred Sloan began producing "cars for every purse and purpose," with each GM car and truck division focusing on a specific socio-economic group, image and price range (the "mass class" theory). GM's theory was based on one of Alfred Sloan's key core strategies—the annual model change, a phenomenon we'll look at shortly.

The scope of GM's focus on marketing and new business techniques is best illustrated by the founding of General Motors Acceptance Corporation (GMAC) in 1919. Through GMAC, GM introduced installment plan buying to an industry that had, up until this time, been strictly COD. By 1925, three of four new GM cars were being purchased "on time." Installment buying of new cars was the strongest evidence of Sloan's recognition of a shift in buying focus from price to "income." He recognized that upwardly mobile buyers desired more expensive, higher prestige cars, and if ownership of these products could be treated as a percentage of the buyer's income, rather than just a one-time cost, then purchases over longer time periods would be acceptable and popular. GM read the marketplace right. Installment buying quickly helped close the gap on Ford, and created a new source of profit through interest on the borrowed purchase price.

After World War I ended, 1919 and 1920 saw a serious economic depression. A number of things contributed to this slump and as a result, events took place in General Motors that would change the company and the course of American business forever.

Used cars, a new phenomenon in the young industry, became a major contributor to the slump, since the industry had not planned a strategy to cope with aging models needing replacement. (This would become part of Sloan's strategy in the first GM "reengineering.") Another, more critical, problem was that Durant had used virtually all the corporation's capital in his ambitious expansion plans, buying some 30 new companies in less than three years.

In 1920, in the face of imminent bankruptcy for a badly overextended General Motors, Pierre Dupont and J.P. Morgan led a contingent that ousted Durant for the second time. Alfred Sloan, a brilliant young MIT graduate and the head of United Motors (that later became Hyatt Roller Bearing) was chosen to become a Director and Vice-President and to design General Motors' first reengineering process between 1920 and 1926. In the process of redesigning GM, Alfred Sloan would design the modern corporation and reinvent the science of marketing. He would be named president of the company in 1923 and run it (with a more benevolent, but just as powerful hand as Ford ran Ford Motor Company) until his death in 1966.

As noted earlier, Sloan identified the "price-to-income" shift that took place in the early 1920s, while Henry Ford did not. As a result, Chevrolet Division outsold Ford for the first time in 1927 by selling 1.7 million "490" Chevrolets. Ford had stayed with the one-model/ lowest-price strategy too long. The switch to the new Model-A in 1927 came too late, causing the Highland Park plant to be shut down for nearly six months and causing Ford to lose sales leadership to Chevy.

In another major development of this period, the "Big Two" became the "Big Three." Walter P. Chrysler had managed the Buick Division of GM from 1910-1920. He became known and respected as GM's best businessman, marketer, and manager under Durant. When Chrysler's contract expired in 1920, and having seen his mentor ousted for the second time, he made the decision to strike out on his own. Walter Chrysler started on the path of building his own auto company by taking over Maxwell Motor Company in 1922. He went on to produce the B-70 under the Chrysler name in 1924. The B-70 got its name by being tested for 50,000 miles at 70 miles per hour. It was to become widely known as the best "quality-engineered" car of the 1920s, and became the foundation on which Chrysler Corporation built its reputation for engineering excellence. Walter Chrysler went on to buy John and Horace Dodge's company in 1928. And in 1928 he introduced the DeSoto, which sold 81,065 units in its first year, an initial model-year record that would stand for 30 years.

As the industry's second decade came to a close, Alfred Sloan's plan for the new General Motors would lift the company to industry and world leadership.

Chapter 3

Emergence of the GM Strategy (1926-1941)

GM Under Sloan

Under Alfred P. Sloan, GM set the standard for the modern corporation. At the core of Sloan's concept were two key principles:

1. "Command," or the development and administration of policy to govern the corporation, should be centralized.

2. "Control," or the independent operations that make up the corporations business units (or Divisions) should be decentralized.

In a manner totally different from Ford, Alfred Sloan's top priorities were styling, sales, marketing and finance. And unlike Ford or his predecessor William Durant, Sloan viewed government and the financial community as key business partners. Some of the most important features of his design for GM were:

*   There would be three principal structures in the company's organization: Operations (the car and truck divisions), Financial Staff, and the General Advisory Staffs (research, marketing, administrative, public relations).

- There would be a central accounting system with overall control of budget and resources allocation. (In Durant's holding company, there was no standard accounting system, and it was virtually impossible to know where the business stood financially).

- Pricing overlaps between the products of the different divisions (Chevrolet, Oakland, Buick, Oldsmobile, Cadillac) would be eliminated, so that each division would serve a unique segment of the market.

- The corporation would be managed by three committees: General Technical, Interdivisional, and Executive. But, they would not countermand the independence of the divisions (the "command/control" principle) to design and market their own, unique products to their assigned markets.

One of Alfred Sloan's top priorities in the first "GM reengineering" was to equip the company to run at a profit in weak economic cycles as well as in good times. To do this, he needed a plan to run the GM assembly plants at a break-even level that was well below their maximum production capacity.

Sloan called on Donaldson Brown, a GM vice-president with great expertise in both mathematics and mass-production technology. Brown designed an approach that he called the "Standard Volume Plan." This plan accomplished all the objectives Sloan had assigned:

- It assumed the plants would be profitable at an average level of 80% capacity, and that flow of products through the Dealer Network would be controlled to accept this rate regardless of overall demand change.

- It allowed price to be based on operating cost rather than competition (a feature that would lead to anti-trust concerns three decades later).

- It ensured a 20% return-on-investment over five-year spans.

In addition to the "Standard Volume Plan" and the "command-control" restructuring of GM into independent operating divisions under standard policy and administration, Sloan's plan for General Motors included other important features.

The annual model change. This was a new approach that also evolved a used-car management strategy. The annual model change called for the company to release new models, with styling updates and key technology innovations, each year. Sloan's objectives for these model changes were to raise prices annually; lower costs (particularly by amortizing tooling costs through equipment that could be used for at least five years); create demand through intense advertising and "class-prestige" consciousness; recycle products by taking in trades and establishing a used-car sales strategy; and using the GMAC installment plan to finance purchases—creating a further profit opportunity through interest payments.

"Cradle-to-grave" philosophy. Basically, it separated the buying population into five segments, graphically portrayed as a pyramid with Chevrolet as the broad-base entry-level for first-time and younger buyers at the lower end of the income scale, and Cadillac as the much narrower "peak," representing the ultimate in prestige and luxury for the middle-aged affluent executive and professional buyer. Along the way, as buyers grew in income and desired a higher profile image and social-status, they would progress from Chevy to Oakland (later Pontiac), to Buick, then Oldsmobile, and finally to Cadillac. This strategy was a sophisticated expansion of Durant's earlier approach, and it would become, more than any other Sloan concept, the basis for GM's long-range success.

Sloan's view of the Dealer as the start of the marketing chain was different from Henry Ford's. Sloan saw the Dealer as one of the most important elements of GM's core strategy. So he placed a major emphasis on developing GM's Dealer organization and on ensuring profitability for the GM Dealer. Specifically, Sloan's Dealer strategy included:

- A planned return-on-investment for the Dealer of at least 15%.

- The dealership as the focus of developing the division's brand image.

- Implementation of the Dealer Operating Report, an element of the GM Standard Accounting System. This was one of Sloan's more important innovations. For the first time, an automaker would be aware of the exact performance of each retail outlet on a monthly basis. And it would provide Dealers with the key tool for managing their day-to-day operations and for longer term forecasting and planning.

- Regular, personal communications with his Dealers. Sloan established regular five-day 15-Dealer trips to ensure that he could keep his finger on the pulse of the marketplace. He valued Dealer input as one of his most important sources of market intelligence. And he made establishing a strong whole-sale contact organization that called on and assisted Dealers in managing their businesses a top GM priority. The result was to make a GM franchise the most valuable in the industry and to establish the Dealer as a key element in the marketing process.

Sloan's plan called for bringing diversification to General Motors as a further hedge against economic cycles and to expand profit opportunity. He added radio, aircraft and airline ownership, banking, diesel engines, commercial trucks, and refrigeration to the corporation's holdings. As an important part of his diversification strategy, Sloan added government contract sales, particularly in commercial trucks. This uniquely GM strategy would become particularly important to the company during the Great Depression of the 1930s.

The Dealer contact process was just one element of a broad **market research function** that Alfred Sloan added to the GM central staffs. He felt that, as the industry grew and became more segmented and complex, customer demands would also grow. In his plan, it was vital that GM have better knowledge of these changes and requirements than did its competitors. And Sloan knew that this research process would have to encompass a means of capturing detailed customer input, as well as Dealer input, and that it would have to chart change in population and demographics of each market served by GM. Market segmentation is the division of the market by needs, price ranges, and different images of the automobile and its purpose and role beyond basic transportation. One of the first results of the

GM market-segmentation was to expand GM's sales across a very wide range of buyers.

Remember that all of Sloan's innovation and change for General Motors was meant to build and support the "cradle-to-grave" marketing concept. So it's important to understand the fundamentals of this strategy in order to understand GM's direction and success between 1923 and 1983. As we've noted, Sloan's concept was an expansion of the earlier strategy developed by William Durant before World War I. Durant's view of the future of the auto industry varied greatly from Henry Ford's. Early in Ford's highly successful manufacturing-price period, Durant predicted very accurately the growth and change in the marketplace. He saw that the automobile would come to mean far more than basic transportation, that it would become, along with the home, the most important element in defining upward social mobility and self-image. Sloan characterized Durant's vision as "a car for every purse and purpose." In that statement he recognized several things: that there would be a shift from price only to percent-of-income in considering an automotive purchase, that the automobile would signify more than just basic transportation, and that it would become an important part of defining the owner's status in society. With that recognition, GM would take a quantum leap past Ford in planning for the future.

Some of the most important features of the "cradle-to-grave" concept are:

- It was based on the concept of "pyramid segmentation," from broad-based entry-level, through more affluent population layers, to the affluent.

- There was to be no price overlap from one division to the next.

- Each division evolved unique styling for each product line. Sloan felt this was the most important key for establishing brand image—matching the owner's social status and lifestyle, to a specific GM product line.

- The process, from entry level to ultimate luxury, would flow from Chevrolet to Cadillac, with each operating division targeting a specific demographic market segment layer.

- There was a specific advertising campaign and overall marketing strategy for each division, designed to align with the image and needs of the market segment(s) served by the division. Ultimately, each division would retain its own advertising agency and take responsibility for developing its marketing/advertising strategy to best address its assigned marketplace.

The goal of the "cradle-to-grave" strategy was to saturate **all** market segments, providing GM with a leadership position throughout the whole automotive marketplace. It was also meant to provide a strong hedge for GM against economic change. Alfred Sloan was one of the first business leaders to foresee the Great Depression, and much of his business strategy was designed to carry the company through the catastrophic economic and social change he foresaw. As we'll see, his strategy worked very well for GM. Finally, the "cradle-to-grave" marketing strategy was the first evidence that the industry was aware of the "voice-of-the-customer." This became an important reason for GM to reevaluate the importance of the strategy in the 1990s.

By 1929, the United States was ending one of the most prosperous economic growth decades in its history. The country had nearly completed the shift from a agricultural to an industrial society, and the automobile was clearly at the forefront of the change. Eighty-five percent of all automotive production was in the U.S., and the oil age had replaced the coal age, shifting the world's trade focus from England to America. But some clouds were forming over the seemingly endless prosperity. For the first time, production was outstripping the rate of growth of the middle class, and the industry saw supply exceed demand. And there were important economic changes taking place.

It's important to note that several factors (in addition to the supply/demand shift) were fundamental in leading to the stock market crash and subsequent economic collapse that began in October, 1929.

- Margin buying of stock had reached a ratio of 50:1; For every dollar an investor put up, he could borrow up to $50 to purchase stock shares.

- Interest rates had exceeded 20%.

- The American farmer had been experiencing economic collapse that began in the mid-1920s.

- The impact of U.S. trade isolation and of tariffs on foreign imports was creating a strong backlash.

All of these factors finally peaked in late 1929, and banks began calling in massive margin notes. A wave of stock sell-offs immediately followed, collapsing the financial markets and the national banking system by early 1930. The Great Depression, that would last until the start of World War II in 1941, had begun.

Fortunately, by 1929, most of Alfred Sloan's restructuring of General Motors was in place, and while both GM and Ford were to see huge cutbacks in employment and business activity, the new structure and marketing strategy would carry the company through the depression years with consistent profit and, ultimately, with strong growth.

The depression of the 1930s was a period of retrenchment, refinement, and finally, recovery for the auto industry. One of its first consequences was a new emphasis on the importance of the retail service and parts business, and on the used vehicle business, as owners shifted their priorities to vehicle maintenance and less expensive used car purchases to cope with the lack of jobs and income. This focus on the retail service and parts (fixed) operation to carry Dealers and company alike in hard times was a feature that would continue long beyond the depression.

A number of changes swept the industry in the 1930s that would remain and continue to shape the business for decades after the Great Depression:

- GM redefined the management of the corporation and all business practices—fundamental changes that would reach far beyond the automotive industry.

- Ford would finally recognize the importance of marketing. The Model-A in 1927, the V-8 engine in 1932 (Henry's last design), and Edsel Ford's restructuring of the company would equip Ford Motor Company to cope with the depression and to return to growth and profit by the mid-1930s.

- At Chrysler Corporation, Walter P. Chrysler would expand his focus on technology and engineering in less expensive products as well as top-end offerings, borrowing from Sloan's strategy.

- Many financial innovations developed, largely in response to the depression. Among these is the impact installment buying had on the industry, bringing in more buyers and allowing people to buy more expensive automobiles and trucks by spreading the payments over time. The growth of warranties as a means to protect owners financially and lower the cost-of-ownership also evolved in this period. To assist Dealers, floor planning and inventory financing was developed. And finally, a less expensive base-model vehicle with a broad range of options helped the industry respond to the general economic crisis.

The 1930s also saw a number of important technological advances. Closed vehicle bodies, heaters, four-wheel brakes, shatter-proof windshields, safety bumpers, synchromesh transmissions, air cleaners, radios, and the Oldsmobile Hydramatic of 1939—the first practical automatic transmission—were among the more important product developments.

GM's continued growth during 1929 to 1935, a time when many major corporations were failing, was due (in addition to the elements of Alfred Sloan's reengineering of the company already discussed) to heavy reinvestment of GM's large profits from the 1920s. Another important factor was Alfred Sloan's relationship with President Franklin Roosevelt. Through their cooperation and the national Civilian Conservation Corps, the demand for GM's commercial trucks helped both GM and the country's economic recovery in the 1930s.

One of Alfred Sloan's goals was for GM to take the automotive industry lead in market-share and profit within 10 years, a goal set in 1926. The success of his plan for GM made this goal a reality by 1934. Alfred Sloan, more than any other figure in automotive history, brought a great many firsts to the industry. Here are the most significant:

— The "command/control" business structure
— Central Accounting System
— Dealer Operating Report
— Donaldson Brown's "Standard Volume Plan"
— The importance of styling; The GM Art and Color Section (later the Design Staff) under Harley Earl
— The segmentation pyramid
— "Cradle-to-grave" marketing
— "Mass-Class" income-based pricing
— Annual model change
— Installment buying/GM financing
— Trading-up and used car marketing strategy
-- Brand imagery
— Dealer Network evolution based on the growing value of the franchise
— Market research
— Central focus on marketing.

A Maturing Industry Evolves Incrementally

As the 1930s progressed, the major automakers became more and more the principal mirrors of sociological change. The national labor unions were finally recognized by the industry, at GM in 1937 and at Ford in 1941. With the advent of the unions, for the first time, the control of efficiency, cost, quality, and productivity were shared between management and labor. This development would further raise the standard of living of the middle class and help to make much of the economic growth of the post-World War II era possible.

As noted earlier, GM and Sloan put major emphasis on the

importance of the Dealer in the total GM system. The Dealer Network evolved very rapidly, and emerged as one of GM's most important competitive strengths during the 1930s, its sheer size making GM's cars and trucks available to the farthest reaches of the country. And its ability to provide service and parts support became one of the company's most vital depression strategies.

In the important 1926 to 1941 period, the auto industry continued to be manufacturing-driven, as markets continued to grow and the industry continued to mature in spite of the depression. Market-share was clearly a direct function of manufacturing and distribution capacity, and GM was the leader in both areas.

Another important dynamic of the auto industry that developed during this time was the business short-term profitability focus. More than any other industry, the automotive business demands constant cash flow to support a wide range of daily manufacturing and Dealer costs for materials, parts and labor. In response, the business developed a "10 day/30 day culture." The culture became paramount to track performance and costs on these very short intervals. This was especially true because market-share was the function of capacity, and not really longer-term business or marketing strategy. This condition would change dramatically in the mid-1970s.

Chapter 4

From Depression to Prosperity

The War Years (1941-1945)

The advent of World War II in 1941 brought an abrupt end to the depression. To the American auto industry this meant an immediate wartime conversion from automotive production to ships, tanks, planes, and munitions. It also caused a surge in technology growth in engines, transmissions, suspension, steering, and electrical systems.

During the war, from 1941 to 1945, there were no new car models. The emphasis in the industry was on maintenance and repair. As a result, the "automotive fleet" aged, and much of the income supporting the Dealer organization was in service and parts business.

One of the important business developments of the war, which would have a long-term impact on the auto business, was the establishment of the War Production Board. The WPB was the training ground for the birth of a new breed of postwar managers. This group would develop design and production strategies under the intense pressure of wartime that would help to revolutionize the industry in the latter 1940s. Management methods, the early development of computers, new types of production machinery, breakthroughs in materials and safety designs, and development of high performance powertrains were some of the more important contributions.

As always, the wartime economy "suspended" normal business and economic cycles. Suddenly demand reached 100%-plus of capacity. As young men entered the military service by the millions, unemployment changed to a scenario of job demands exceeding labor supply. Thousands of women began to fill the employment void in factories producing war materials. The market environment rapidly became one of more spendable income with less goods and services available. This growing pent-up demand set the stage for the post-war buying boom in the auto industry.

The Golden Age of Excess (1946-1970)

The period from the end of World War II through the mid-1960s was, in many aspects, much like the 1918 to 1929 period following World War I. The 1946 to 1970 period was one of virtually total American economic dominance globally, with very little serious foreign competition in domestic markets for automobiles, computer systems, many other consumer goods areas, and even agriculture.

It was a time of high employment, low taxes (down from their high levels of the war years), low inflation, and plentiful and inexpensive fuel. Prosperity reached all-time highs as the growth of the suburbs in the 40s and 50s and of the two-income family in the 60s strongly sky-rocketed the number of two-car/truck families. The auto industry once again found itself in a position of under capacity, and the business was, more than ever, manufacturing-driven.

General Motors' post-war strategy featured three priorities:

1. Styling.
2. Demand for automatic transmissions.
3. High compression engines.

In the 1950s the industry evolved a uniquely American way of conducting business, from advertising to franchising to shopping. It became a marketing concept that spread worldwide and led to the integrated world economy of the 1990s. The rapid development of the suburbs and multi-car families led, in addition to accelerated market development, to a rapid development in the infrastructure, particularly in the growth of expressways and interstate highways. Between 1950 and 1956, $26 billion were spent in building 41,000 miles of freeways.

The United States became deeply involved in the rebuilding of foreign economies crippled by the war. The country built up a huge trade surplus, all contributing to economic prosperity and the continued strengthening of the auto industry. Quality, social-consumerism and environmental issues were not yet factors. Continually escalating costs could still be readily passed on to consumers.

All in all, this was the most advantageous scenario possible for the automotive industry.

Alfred Sloan's management skill continued to sustain the GM growth position through the 1960s. The annual style model announcements became major media events. Yet much of the change was surface or cosmetic in nature. There was little pressure for significant improvements in fuel efficiency, durability, serviceability, environmental protection technology, and safety—things that would have huge cost impact on the industry in the 1970s. The industry was still in a firm position to pass higher prices on to the consumer. By focusing largely on annual styling change, much of the plant tooling could be preserved, helping to keep the manufacturer's costs down. Research investment costs to the industry were also far below the expensive demands that fuel economy, emissions and safety regulation would place upon them in the 1970s and 80s.

GM was able to strengthen its cradle-to-grave strategy right through the late 1960s. As a result, it increased its market-share to over 60% by the early 1960s. There were also important product advances. The 1949 Ford and the 1955 Chevrolet, for example, brought major breakthroughs in design, engines, body structure, suspensions, and powertrain technology. But in 1955, GM introduced a major marketing innovation to the industry when it brought luxury features to its basic lines, like the Chevrolet BelAir and the Pontiac Bonneville (redesigned in 1955, introduced as a new model in 1958).

The economic prosperity and continuing growth in demand led to the rapid expansion of the company's manufacturing plants and its Dealer Network. It also led to a surge in mass-media electronic advertising and marketing. The industry marketing that Henry Ford had dismissed only 40 years earlier as an unnecessary and foolish waste, had become a multi-billion dollar business responsible for a significant percentage of the country's Gross Domestic Product.

GM's major competitor, Ford Motor Company, found itself in a period of immense change, not unlike that which Sloan brought to GM in the 1920s. Following Henry Ford's death in 1947, the company was being run by Harry Bennett, an ex-boxer who many in the industry considered to be little more than a strong-arm enforcer. Bennett originally came to Ford's attention for his part in the company's early bloody confrontations with Walter Reuther's union forces.

During Henry Ford's final years, he came to rely on Harry Bennett more and more. While this was happening, most of Ford's real automotive managers were being driven from the business, as Bennett consolidated his hold on the company.

Finally, with some help from the Federal Government and the Ford family, Henry Ford II, Ford's grandson, was called back from the Navy to take charge of the company. One of young Henry's first actions was to bring Ernest Breech, a GM vice-president, to Ford Motor Company to become the company's chief of operations, in the hope that he would bring Sloan's management style and strategy to Ford. Ford and Breech next brought in an entire management team from the War Production/Planning Board and the Army Air Corps to take over the direction of the company. This group of young managers would become known as the "Whiz Kids." The Ford "Whiz Kids" included:

- **Charles "Tex" Thornton**—who, after finally leaving Ford, would go on to found Litton Industries. Tex Thornton proved the concept that a true professional manager could manage any enterprise, without special knowledge of its products.

- **Robert S. McNamara**—a brilliant mathematician who became president of Ford in 1960. He would become Secretary of Defense under John F. Kennedy.

- **Franklin C. Reith**—who would leave Ford to start his own business.

- **George C. Moore**—who would also leave Ford to start his own business.

- **J. Edward Lundy**—who became the recruiter to a whole new generation of leaders to Ford, teaching them the "Whiz Kids" systems and philosophies.

- **Arjay R. Miller**—who would also rise to the company presidency, and ultimately would become dean of the Stanford Business School.

- **Ben D. Mills**—who would ultimately become the troubleshooter to "clean up" after the Edsel disaster.

- **James O. Wright**—who resigned to become president of a major Ford Supplier after his contemporary, Arjay Miller, was named president.

- **Charles C. Bosworth**—the only "Whiz Kid" who stayed at Ford for his entire career, and the only one who did not achieve at least the rank of vice-president.

- **William R. Anderson**—who would ultimately become president of Bekins Moving and Storage Company.

This team would lead Ford's transition to a modern financial, marketing and organizational structure. And in a little over five years, they would bring the company from near financial collapse in 1946 back to a position as one of the world's largest and most profitable companies. Under the new management team, the dramatically changed 1949 Ford revolutionized post-war automotive styling and positioned the company for two decades of success.

Another important industry phenomenon of the post-war era was the growth of commercial diesels, particularly in the 1960s. The Cummins, Mack Thermodyne, GM Two Stroke, Perkins, and Volvo Turbo were all important commercial products of this period. Like all areas of the automotive industry, the growth of the commercial "big rigs" exploded with the nation's infrastructure growth.

In the midst of the industry's most positive growth environment ever, there were some dark clouds forming. The first of these involved growing anti-trust pressures on General Motors. The relationship between GM and the DuPont family went back to 1910 when Pierre DuPont served as a Director in partnership with William

Durant. He later became president while new director and vice-president Alfred Sloan conducted his reengineering plan between 1920 and 1923. The DuPont company had always supplied GM with a great many of its chemicals. By the late 1940s, this partnership had become so large that it prompted the early anti-trust discussions related to GM. Then, during the 1950s, GM's market-share exceeded 50% and the anti-trust pressures were accelerated. (Remember the manufacturing-driven formula: share is proportionate to production and distribution capacity.)

Then, by the late 1950s, two other factors added to GM's anti-trust worries. The first was a suit by GM Dealers against GM involving annual refranchising, loading Dealers with inventory they couldn't sell (Remember the Donaldson Brown "Standard Volume Plan" requiring Dealers to regulate flow.), and generally applying extreme pressures to the Dealers to follow what Dealers felt were arbitrary policies. No sooner was that lawsuit settled (largely in favor of the Dealers), than the government became aware that GMAC controlled fully 10% of **all** U.S. financing in 1959.

As a result of these problems, GM took steps to take the anti-trust pressure off the company. First they stretched the intervals between Dealer refranchising from one year to five years, and lightened a number of requirements on the Dealers. And GM took a second step in 1965 centralizing their assembly plants to head off the "break-up GM" push. This became part of the problems of the 1970s and '80s when General Motors Assembly Division (GMAD) was formed.

Another problem that began to have a powerful impact on GM's expenses, productivity and quality was the pattern contracts with the labor unions. Until the advent of the Japanese challenge in the 1970s, the higher cost and other problems these "across the industry" labor contracts cost could be passed on to the customers. After all, prosperity was high and there was no real competitive standard. All these things would change dramatically by the mid-1970s.

Finally, the last "dark cloud" of the 1950s proved to be a predictor of things to come just over a decade later. A funny looking little German compact, the Volkswagen Beetle, that the industry didn't take seriously when it entered the U.S. market a few years earlier, sold 380,000 units in 1958 and captured 10% of the market in 1959. Suddenly everyone took the Beetle very seriously. The introduction of the Chevrolet Corvair, Dodge Dart, Ford Falcon, and Plymouth Valiant in 1959 showed just how seriously.

Other indicators of tougher times to come were sending the industry some strong signals. After Alfred Sloan's death in 1966, General Motors really had no strong seccession plan in place. Like many companies with very long-term, dominant leaders, most of the executives growing up around Sloan were relatively weak clones of the master, and didn't bring his leadership or brilliant mind to the party. Sloan's illustrious career saw him serve as Director and Vice-President from 1920-1923, President from 1923-1937, Chairman from 1937-1956, and Chairman Emeritus from 1956-1966. From the time he entered in 1917 (ironically, when Durant bought his company to get Sloan), Alfred Sloan served GM in a position of top leadership for 50 years. His was a career that would not just redesign GM and bring it to the position of the world's biggest, most profitable company, but would virtually redesign the way corporation(s) worked across **all** industries.

After Sloan's death, GM became very insular with its executives isolated from its markets and customers. It seemed not to recognize the social, economic and competitive change that was taking place in the industry and across the country. Instead, the company was becoming out-of-touch and highly averse to risk and the kind of innovation that had made it great.

During this time, in Japan, a country defeated in World War II and not taken seriously by anyone as a world automotive power before 1970, a "revolution" was taking place. Japan had evolved a national economic plan ("Japan, Inc.") that was designed to provide Japan with ultimate world economic dominance. The plan would be based on quality (a feature Japan had **never** been known for), and the automobile industry would lead the way.

In 1953, the world's leading experts on quality manufacturing methods were from the U.S.; Drs. Deming and Juran. Ironically, they were largely ignored in their own country. Not so in Japan, where they were welcomed with open arms and where Japanese industrialists paid rapt attention to their teachings, and moreover, **implemented** them. By 1970, Japan's auto industry was ready to bring the results of their work to an unsuspecting and unprepared American auto industry.

The final blow came in 1965, when an obsessive consumer champion named Ralph Nader published a book called *Unsafe at Any Speed* attacking Chevrolet's Corvair in particular, and the safety performance of the U.S. automobile industry in general. It was to be the opening shot in an all-out consumerism attack on the industry that would play a major role in the push for federal regulation in the 1970s and 1980s. An unsuspecting industry was poised for the greatest change in its history.

Chapter 5

The Shift to Market-Driven (1971-1983)

The Priorities Shift of the 1970s

By the early 1970s, America had grown largely dependent on foreign oil. And most of this oil was controlled by the Organization of Petroleum Export Countries or "OPEC," which was in turn, largely controlled by Arab nations that did not have (with the exception of Saudi Arabia and Iran of the pre-Ayatollah Khomeini era) strong political ties to the U.S. In 1973, the first of two "Arab Oil Crises" (the second came in 1979) hit the country, dramatically cutting the supply of oil and greatly increasing its cost. Very suddenly, the component that had protected the manufacturing-driven auto industry for 70 years—cheap, readily available oil—was no longer either cheap or readily available. The results were catastrophic. The 1973 oil crisis spearheaded a shift in virtually all the priorities of the industry. Most significant were:

- Fuel economy was now a definite design limiter, and with fuel precious and expensive, a top customer priority.

- Government intervention, combined with the parallel consumerism and environmentalism movements, made economy, safety and emissions controls mandated requirements and major cost impactors.

68

- Quality awareness, driven by the influx of very high quality Japanese product, was a definite customer priority.

- Underhood technology, particularly fuel systems, emissions systems, crash worthiness, and serviceability and durability features began undergoing extensive redesign.

- Cost containment, facing the dual pressures of Japanese competition and a rapidly developing unfriendly economic environment (featuring double-digit inflation and interest, higher taxes, and lower investment incentives), became a top priority. Every aspect of cost—labor, parts, supplier costs, medical and retirement costs, and advertising—came under intense scrutiny.

- Labor union growth, particularly "pattern" cross-industry contracts that had done so much to raise the average American's standard of living, were suddenly a significant problem in the new cost-competitive marketplace.

- The rapid cost increases caused by new demands in design, engineering, tooling componentry, and research to meet mandated and competitively-driven requirements, which had traditionally been passed on to consumers, were now causing a new phenomenon called "sticker-shock."

- The effect of electronic media on an industry suddenly under intense, unfriendly scrutiny brought national focus to stories like Chevy engines used in other divisions' products, the Volvo transmission "scare," the Ford Pinto "exploding" gas tank, and GM's full-size (C/K) pick-up gas tank stories.

The most important impact of all was the sudden, dramatic shift to a market-driven industry, a shift almost universally missed by U.S. manufacturers. Inflation, high interest rates and taxation were joining far higher gasoline prices to make the total cost-of-ownership (fuel, maintenance, insurance, finance, and basic vehicle price) prohibitive. With the new standard of competition offered by high quality Japanese products, parts cost and availability become key competitive factors. They were the basic impactors on customer satisfaction and service/serviceability priorities brought about by the late 70s recession, emissions, and economic issues.

The Japanese Challenge

The first Japanese entries in U.S. markets in the 1960s were sub-standard products like the Toyota Crown. American manufacturers didn't give Toyota and Nissan much thought when they set up the first dual dealership operations with (ironically) Detroit-area Dealers. By the mid-1970s, however, several things became painfully obvious—the Japanese produced a very competitive, high quality product; they could make a small car that was profitable and would capture significant market-share; and they were clearly here to stay!

By 1976, Japanese products were cheaper and of higher quality, and they offered higher fuel economy, lower operating costs, and better responses to the new customer priorities. Toyota pioneered lean manufacturing techniques, much as Henry Ford did seventy years earlier. Japan's geography and culture gave them natural leads in some key areas, particularly in small cars and efficiency and effective use of teams. And they brought innovative new techniques to the marketplace. For example, Toyota studied supermarket operations, particularly the interaction between customers and "stockers" to learn the fundamentals of "pull" marketing—requirements driven by the customer and marketplace and not dictated by manufacturers.

As part of their national economic strategy, the Japanese began production facility investments in foreign target markets, including the U.S. This strategy combined: building of large-scale foreign assembly plants, wholesale movements of their parts/components affiliates (Keiretsu concept), investment in American bond markets, strong interaction with local employes and parts suppliers, and political interaction into target countries. The goal was to create the aura of an "American company" around the Japanese firm.

The Japanese "formula" following the oil crisis was to focus on absolute leadership in:

- Fuel economy
- Quality
- Price
- Reliability
- An image as an American supplier.

To build profitable compact cars, the Japanese extended the logic of the 1955 Chevy BelAir—offering luxury options on well designed base models.

Toyota's strategy focused strongly on these four elements:

1. Kaizen (continuous improvement)
2. Kanban (just-in-time parts availability)
3. Employe Teams
4. **Control** of quality through **people**, and not by "inspection," the traditional approach.

Between 1970 and 1980, Japanese market-share grew rapidly, heading toward their long-range target of 10% globally.

The Domestic Industry Threatened

In the late 1970s, as customer demands intensified in all areas of product and service, driven by intense competition and the expanded choice this competition offered, the "Big Three" domestic manufacturers found themselves in a state of crisis. Ford and Chrysler were both nearing the brink in financial solvency, driven by financial losses in the worst economy since the depression. Here's how the basic situation looked:

- The domestic automakers lost $4.2 billion and production was down by seven million units in 1980.

- Chrysler, under new Chairman Lee Iacocca, turned to the Federal Government for assistance, which responded with the Chrysler Loan Guarantee Act for $1.5 billion.

- Ford's losses caused a major reorganization and a "reinventing" of the product around the Taurus.

- GM posted their first annual loss in 60 years.

- Japanese share climbed to 21.2% of the market, and their top manufacturers, Toyota, Honda and Nissan had high market acceptance in all customer priority areas.

In response to this deep, dramatic change in the industry and its lost profits and market-share, GM launched its second major reorganization in 1983. These were the major components of the GM restructuring:

- Strong focus was placed on automation, particularly in robotics with dedicated robotics-based plants at Orion, Poletown, Buick City, and Wentzville, Ohio.

- Three product-groups were formed: Chevrolet-Pontiac-GM Canada (CPC), Buick-Oldsmobile-Cadillac (BOC), and Truck and Bus, with a focus on cross-division common product platforms.

- Acquisitions were made outside the core-business: EDS in 1984 for $2.5 billion, and Hughes Electronics in 1985 for $5.0 billion, along with the acquisition of Lotus.

- GMAC expanded into additional financial markets including home mortgages.

- GMAD's assembly plants were reorganized under the groups.

- Huge capital commitments were made to plant automation and robotics ($45-70 billion in investments.)

- The S-Car program, later to become Saturn, was launched.

- An extensive retraining contract was signed with the UAW to support retraining of employes replaced by automation to become robotics operations and repair technicians.

The results of their massive reorganization were, for the most part, negative to General Motors. The most harmful results were these:

- Loss of brand image and equity due to lost image alignment between divisions and traditional markets.

- Overlapping products and pricing that served to confuse markets.

- Generally poor quality products.

- Serious accounting system breakdowns.

- Weakened capital position.

- Very poor employe morale.

- Slowed response-times to markets and customers.

- No real product strategies in key segments, particularly mid-size sedans and minivans.

- General deterioration of the Dealer Network (and Dealer morale).

- Perhaps most important, GM lost their traditional marketing anchor—the cradle-to-grave strategy.

The one strong, positive result was the Saturn experience, which is now becoming the basis for GM's third reengineering based on building customer enthusiasm.

GM found itself the high-cost producer in an extremely cost-sensitive market, with the longest development cycles and the highest labor costs—a huge challenge for the organization as it entered the 1990s.

The "Big Three" Address Change

General Motors, Ford and Chrysler each found themselves faced with the most significant competitive and strategic challenges in their history. Not only were all of the market and customer priorities that had defined the auto business for its first 75 years changing, and changing rapidly, but there was a group of foreign suppliers seemingly ready and able to meet the new requirements faster and better than the domestic companies. And the "Big Three" were being called on to make quick, dramatic change at a time when they were suffering huge financial losses, the first such losses since the depression of the 1930s. Each automaker took a unique approach in responding to the challenges. Let's briefly summarize each.

GM. We've looked at the GM reorganization strategy of 1983-84 in some detail. This was GM's second major organization-wide restructuring paralleling Sloan's effort of the early 1920s in scope and importance. In a nutshell, the GM approach involved restructuring into three common-platform groups, a massive infusion of (**very** expensive) plant automation, and diversifying to add systems and electronics capability in a vertical integration move. GM clearly chose process innovation over product development, and a technology focus over reengineering the way people do their work. The plan simply didn't work. (As mentioned, the introduction of the Saturn process as a "laboratory" for reinventing the business was the one, significant positive.)

The most damaging cost to the company, beyond financial loss and the disruption and loss of many good people, was the loss of the core strategy that GM built its business on—cradle-to-grave. The traditional, unique brand image and brand equity that defined each GM division and gave the company the broadest range of customers of any manufacturer in the industry was, for all intents and purposes, gone. This loss would be so devastating to the company that only 10 years later, it would cause the biggest executive shake-up since Durant in 1920, and would lead to a third major reengineering, now underway.

The final chapter and the last section of this book will examine this current effort in detail and analyze what it must do to solidify returning GM to world leadership.

Ford. Being smaller than GM and with less investment capital, Ford reached crisis faster and harder than General Motors (but not as fast or traumatically as Chrysler). While not as near bankruptcy as Chrysler, Ford found itself in a position of deep financial loss and with a product portfolio sadly inadequate to meet the new market priorities and superior-quality Japanese products of 1980.

Ford's response was totally different from GM's. In fact, their lack of investment capital may have been the best thing that could have happened to them. It forced them to focus on people and on a shorter, less expensive product design cycle. They simply couldn't afford to take GM's approach with its focus on expensive automation assembly plant rebuilding, and vertical acquisition of non-core companies. And this probably saved Ford from extinction.

Ford put its first priority on people and on new business processes to ensure improved quality ("Job 1"). By taking this approach, they evolved a set of strategies very similar to Toyota. More productive work teams were formed, and they in turn developed more efficient business processes. The Ford focus on "intellectual capital" worked for them, and worked well.

Next, Ford focused on product, specifically on the mid-size family sedan and on a profitable, high quality compact—products that would compete heads-up with Accord, Camry, and Corolla. And they used their new team approach to attack the problem with the now famous "Team Taurus." The Taurus gave Ford two absolute keys to survival and turn-around: a core product that would be perceived as the equal of the very best Japanese offerings, and a process for product development that was faster and cheaper—two absolute priorities for the 1990s. Concurrently, the compact Escort proved a powerful entry into the high fuel-efficient categories. Unlike its domestic predecessors, (cars like Pinto, Vega, and Chevette), the Escort was in every way a well thought out, unique, top-quality product that was affordable and that met a surprisingly broad range of segment needs.

So, in the end, Ford's financial weakness and desperate need to develop two competitive, quality, profitable products for key segments not only saved the company, but positioned it strongly to be a successful player entering the 1990s.

Another important point that should be made is that when GM and Ford began an in-depth examination of Toyota in 1979, they came up with two different conclusions. GM saw Toyota as not really running their assembly plants much differently than the domestics did. Their conclusion was that GM could get a clear advantage in productivity and quality if they became world leaders in technology of plant automation, particularly in the evolving technology of robotics. For a number of reasons, this strategy didn't work. First, it was **very** costly. The technology of the early 1980s in robotics was not nearly where it should have been to justify a virtually total commitment to it as the central production strategy. And perhaps most important, the GM team missed a most important point: Toyota **was** using revolutionary manufacturing process, but **not** in terms of cutting-edge technology. Instead, their use of cross-function teams, their empowerment of workers to take control of quality on the job floor, and their basic business philosophy of continuous improvement were their "secrets." Mostly because they couldn't afford to take the costly automation approach, Ford stumbled into the same secrets!

Chrysler. By 1980, Chrysler had reached the financial brink. Forced to turn to the Federal Government for the capital needed to survive bankruptcy, like Ford, Chrysler couldn't afford to take the more expensive capital equipment investment approach to restructuring. So, unlike GM, Chrysler fell back on what historically had made them successful—engineering, and the issues surrounding product engineering: development cycle-times and restructured cross-function design teams.

But, engineering excellence and reduced development times and costs, alone, would not have been enough to save Chrysler, not in an environment where the Japanese competitors were perceived to have the winning combination of quality and superior customer service. Chrysler needed something less tangible, but every bit as vital as productivity, engineering, and more efficient process. They needed an **image**, credibility, and most important, they needed the emotional support of the American public.

Chrysler got all these things through the leadership and charisma of their new Chairman, Lee Iacocca. Iacocca was the perfect profile for Chrysler, a well-known "car-guy," who'd been cast aside by Ford, an underdog, a tough guy and a fighter who was known as being honest and unwilling to quit. And, perhaps most important, he was a first-class salesman who could communicate. Lee Iacocca **became** Chrysler, and he made Chrysler into a symbol of an America besieged by foreign competition. He made the fight personal; he attacked the Japanese and took a "national pride" approach. "Buy American" became synonymous with "Buy Chrysler." And he took the philosophy a step further. He wanted the public to buy Chrysler because he truly felt it to be a superior, quality product. "If you can find a better car than a Chrysler, buy it" won the hearts of the public and almost singlehandedly mounted a buy American backlash. Lee Iacocca was the perfect man for the job for Chrysler in the 1980s. He quite literally **became** American business.

Iacocca's management skills in reengineering Chrysler were, of course, important. He was a forceful figure in changing Chrysler's culture. In moving the company from a monolithic, classic, vertical bureaucracy to efficient cross-function teams, he was also the right man in creating and "becoming" the marketing image for Chrysler, a new image that **also** captured the company's traditional strength—excellence in engineering.

Toyota. While this section is about the responses of the domestic Big Three to the challenges of the 1970s and the shift to a market-driven auto industry, it is a good idea to review Toyota Motor Company, the leading Japanese competitor and, in many ways the benchmark of the period. Toyota's strategy was based on a "lean manufacturing" concept that had four major components.

First is "Kaizen," or continuous improvement. Continuous improvement means, simply, constantly reviewing every process and system for incremental improvements. It prizes constantly getting better in many small, but important, ways over the occasional innovative leap; it's more about singles than home runs. Second, is "Kanban" or Just-in-Time parts availability. This means keeping the cost of expensive inventory down by just using the components that are needed, **when** they're needed. It's also meant to improve quality by focusing attention on a smaller inventory and placing the responsibility for review on the work floor and at the part's source, instead of in the inspection room. The third element of the Toyota strategy revolved around employe teams. Toyota was probably the first manufacturer to make widespread use of cross-function, highly empowered work teams in every aspect of product design and production. And, most important, these teams were fully empowered to modify and improve process without all the bureaucratic reviews and approvals that process change typically involves. The fourth factor of the Toyota strategy is really the foundation for the others—the positioning of **people** as the company's most important resource. However empowerment of people means nothing unless the organization is willing to invest in its people, and place its trust in them. In other words, the business must prepare its managers and workers to execute empowerment in a responsible and productive manner. Toyota had made this investment in, and this commitment to its people. Further, the motivation, communications process and feedback system the company used was carefully designed to support its people.

Japanese Strategy—The Domestic View

To complete the picture of the industry between the late 1970s and mid-1980s, it's necessary to look at how American manufacturers viewed the Japanese automotive industry's strategy for the U.S. (and world) markets.

The first element of this strategy was Japan's focus on market-share over quality. We've seen that Toyota had a stated goal of 10% of the global market by 2000. Remember that in 1980, the position of the dollar and yen were virtually reversed from what they are today. When combined with the strong dollar of the period, cheaper Japanese labor, and more efficient process, Japan had a definite cost advantage. It was the contention of domestic manufacturers that the Japanese automakers used this advantage, combined with their market-share goal to sell certain products in the U.S. at less than cost, a process called "dumping." In other words, it was felt that Japan was literally buying market-share to gain market footholds in the U.S.

The second element of the Japanese strategy was to export process. Toyota, Honda, Nissan and Mazda all made major commitments to plant construction in the U.S. during the 1980s. This initiative included several actions. First, it involved very large investment in local facility construction. Second, it involved transporting many elements of the Japanese "Keiretsu" to the U.S.—the Japanese suppliers, banks, and affiliate businesses who share stock ownership (cross-companies) with the manufacturer. Third, it included qualifying and using a significant number of American domestic parts suppliers. This was an important part of the Japanese manufacturers' tactic of casting themselves as an "American car company," of making themselves a fully functioning part of and contributor to the American economy. As part of this approach, all the Japanese manufacturers make a strong point of becoming "good corporate citizens" and making large philanthropic contributions to local causes. For example, Toyota and Honda are the largest corporate contributors to National 4-H Council, one of the country's largest youth development organizations.

While the Japanese were employing this strategy to export process and become a fully-functioning American-based manufacturer, American industry contended that the Japanese were actively working to block American exports into Japan—the "level playing field" issue. As a result of these charges, the Japanese initiated a system of voluntary export restraints limiting the volume of cars and trucks they exported into the U.S. market. At best, these restraints and the current Japanese recession and political upheaval, which have taken away their cost advantage, can be viewed as temporary opportunities for the U.S. industry to significantly improve its competitive position. The approach the U.S. must follow is the subject of the final section of this book.

Chapter 6

Recession and Reengineering (1983-1991)

The early eighties saw the auto industry focus virtually all of its efforts on quality—both perceived and real. And, the Japanese were the clear early leaders in quality. GM, Ford, and Chrysler all responded strongly, while in very different ways, to this challenge. As a result the domestic manufacturers closed the quality gap, and in many areas, matched or exceeded the Japanese in quality by 1990. As so often happens in situations like this, the marketing focus on quality was so great and the expenditures so intense, that by the early nineties, quality had ceased being a "competitive differentiator"—a wall to set yourself apart from competition—and had become an "entry level" concern, a game ante for doing business.

An interesting aspect of the quality race in the automobile business is the "halo effect." This means simply that the **first** competitor to develop a reputation for being best in an area, like quality, regardless of how well others respond, will **always** be viewed by most people as being the best. This was certainly the case in automobile and truck quality. Even though independent reviewers like J.D. Power consistently rate American makers as good as or even better than their Japanese counterparts, large numbers of buyers still perceive Japanese products as being of superior quality.

By the late 1980s, the ultra-competitive automobile industry had completed the shift to being market-driven and had shifted its focus to the customer as its most important concern. In fact, the "voice-of-the-customer," the term for determining customer requirements at the input to each process, had become an industry obsession.

Customer satisfaction had long been a concern of the industry. Most commonly measured by CSi, the "Customer Satisfaction Index," customer satisfaction had for some time been used as a measure for Dealer recognition and as a means of grading manufacturers and their products. The index included measures of product quality, delivery, Dealer Sales, Service, Warranty, and overall treatment of the customer. Over time, it had come to focus strongly on retail performance, and to be used as a source for Dealer recognition, and (at times) for Dealer punishment.

Toyota, Lexus and Nissan, Infiniti had taken almost complete control of the customer satisfaction index ratings until the late 1980s. Then, the one strong positive result of the mid-80s restructuring, the Saturn, made a dramatic impact on the industry. In a very short time, Saturn took over leadership in practically every CSi category, and in the process, brought a new term to the business—customer enthusiasm. While customer satisfaction talked about **responding** to the customer, customer enthusiasm talked about proactively understanding the customer's needs. Then, it became a measure of consistently exceeding those needs—of "delighting" the customer.

The industry's marketing, advertising, and public relations mechanisms swing into high gear in all-out campaigns to tout each manufacturer's efforts and performance in focusing on the customer. In- and outbound 800 lines were set up by every division of GM to make it easy for the customer to resolve problems, and for the division to measure customer reactions to its products and its service performance. Executives became more directly involved with the customer in a number of ways. And Dealer focus shifted strongly toward understanding and responding to the customer, and to offering a wide range of conveniences designed to make it far easier for the customer to do business with the company.

One of the most important features of the changing focus on the customer was to bring customer concern to the attention of **every** function of the business. Historically, customer satisfaction had been the "job" of the Service organization, both at the Dealer level and at the manufacturer's marketing divisions. As long as the concern for the customer was isolated in the fixed operations end of the business, it would not receive the focus and support required to drive real change. Saturn made the customer **everyone's** concern—the designer, the assembly-line worker, the engineer, the plant manager, the Sales-Service-Parts reps, the Union, the retailer (Dealer) and every retail employe. It accomplished this by going far beyond the marketing and advertising process. Instead, it built measures and rewards around identifying and responding to its customers' needs and expectations. And in the process, it virtually reinvented the business. In the closing section of this book and in Section IV on the customer, we'll examine these strategies for customer enthusiasm in detail.

In other areas of the industry, technology was accelerating rapidly throughout the 1980s. Fuel and emissions management systems had become computer-electronically controlled. And computer control had made driveability a far more precise science than it was only a decade earlier. ABS braking systems and traction-control combined with air bags to make handling and safety much better than they were in the 1970s. Shock-absorbing bodies and frames and a wave of new materials made cars and trucks much safer **and** more durable than the previous generations of products. Overall, cars and trucks were safer, more reliable, more durable, more serviceable, handled and rode better, and performed far better by 1991 than they had in 1980.

The "downside" of technological change was felt on the retail cost side of the business where the costs of training, equipment, and facilities all skyrocketed during the decade. All these things brought attention to an area that will become a top priority in the 1990s, the Dealer's cost to retail a unit.

By 1989, the country was experiencing an economic recession, as were Japan and Europe. The weak economy made the problems experienced by the auto industry even worse, as sales and profits were again falling. This combination of a weak economy, high cost and falling market-share put extreme pressure on General Motors to downsize, cut all of its costs, and take whatever measures necessary to return the company to profitability. As the company entered the 1990s the clear priorities were **lower unit-cost** (GM was and is the high-cost producer), **reengineering** the business throughout, **faster and less expensive cycle-times**, and the **customer**.

Section II.   The Automotive Dealer

Chapter 1

All About Dealers

The Early Ford Dealer

Let's take a look at how the automotive Dealer concept was born and developed by Ford Motor Company, which established the early pattern for the industry.

- By 1907, Ford began installing its factory branches, and in turn, the Dealers' outlets that those branches served.

- Ford's original requirements for its Dealers were that they be "financially strong, of good standing in the community, have presentable homes, and agree to handle Fords only." As he did for his assembly plant workers, Henry Ford established strict requirements for the Dealers of his products.

- The Ford Motor Car dealership was considered to be of such great value (as a desirable business holding) that Dealers who owned them were required to follow strict orders from Highland Park and the Dealer's branch office. With upwards of 1,000,000 Model-Ts a year being produced by 1915, no demands were considered too strict to offset the desire of the businessman to own the coveted and valuable Ford dealership.

- The branch offices quickly became the equivalent of today's Zones, and were managed by the best Dealers, hired by Ford (somewhat the equivalent of today's mega-Dealer concept).

- Each branch controlled all Dealers in their marketing area, and made contracts with Dealers and Agencies.

- Ford quickly gave the factory-managed branches control of service standards in dealerships, and the control of all sales contracts.

- Ford's 11 branches more than doubled in 1910, with veteran Dealers hired to run them.

- The branch offices also housed parts for all Dealers in their area (an idea that may have renewed value in tomorrow's markets).

- The early Ford distribution strategy was strictly a "push-marketing" approach, meaning the factory's requirement to distribute as much of its capacity as possible (and not market demand) was the driver. And given the rapid growth market and Ford's leadership, the "push" strategy was, without question, correct for its time.

- By the end of 1912 there were more than 7,000 Ford Dealers. And although buyers could purchase their new Model-Ts directly from Highland Park, Branches/Dealers were out-selling the factory by three to one. Dealers' volume would rise to 88% of all Ford sales by 1916. The concept of a Dealer-based distribution system had finally taken hold in what had been a factory-direct business.

- By 1913, Ford was mapping markets to assign Dealers. The 7,000 Dealers were served by 46 Branches, and there were three Ford Dealers for every U.S. county. The size of Ford's distribution organization was a dramatic measure of how deeply the automobile was impacting U.S. commerce and the American "industrialization."

- By 1914, Highland Park was sending out factory trainers to teach Dealers service and parts management. This was the birth of the Wholesale Field contact organization, which would later evolve to the franchise industry's most complex support system.

By the time of the U.S. entry into World War I, being an automobile Dealer was widely considered the prime sales job in world industry. Opportunity for profit was guaranteed, and the chance of failure negligible. In spite of the immense size of the early Ford Dealer Network and the great value of the franchise, Henry Ford never came to view the Dealer as a key strategic part of the Ford system. Dealers were more of a "necessary evil" that Ford found harder to control than the factory. Dealers were not treated as true business partners by Ford in the early years of the industry. Control of the factory was purely top-down and Dealer input was not a real element in Ford's business designs.

How GM Treated Dealers

By contrast, Alfred Sloan immediately recognized the strategic importance of his Dealers. As a key element in Sloan's 1920s marketing strategy, he focused strongly on the Dealers to represent the GM "image" and "provide GM levels of service" to the customer. To Sloan (unlike Ford) the Dealer was an obvious extension of the GM image. And as an important part of his strategy, Alfred Sloan spent a great deal of time and effort talking to Dealers and gathering their thoughts on GM products and what customers were looking for. As we've seen in "Historical Perspective," Sloan was also vitally concerned with Dealer profitability as a cornerstone of GM's financial performance. His implementation of the Dealer Operating Report and his personal five-day Dealer contact trips attested to the key role in the GM system that Sloan afforded the Dealer.

Sloan's attention to building the industry's strongest Dealer organization paid off in the years of the depression when the serving and selling strength of the GM Dealers became one of the corporation's most important business assets.

The Dealer As Entrepreneur

Like nearly all successful entrepreneurs, the car/truck Dealer has a very high ego factor (which, as we'll see later, can be a big positive). This means Dealers trust in, and demand strong recognition of their business skills, and tend to be skeptical of others who (they feel) may have lessor skills. The Dealer also tends to assume that, since they are on the "front-line," selling and servicing the product, they know more about the business than the manufacturer whose products they distribute and service. These factors, combined with a long history of disagreement on many product and business issues, have made Dealers often suspicious and distrustful of the factory. Much of this friction can be attributed to the high investment required for ownership. And much is due to various state laws that greatly limit the amount of control a manufacturer can exert in governing a Dealer's franchise requirements. Another issue contributing to friction involves territorial control. Dealers have always desired "protected" market areas where they wouldn't have to compete with their own brand or company. The control issue, when combined with the ego factor and desire for total control, has been a traditional point of contention.

At the same time, Dealers have high expectations in terms of product design and quality, parts support, financial support, and business systems. Competition between manufacturers has driven Dealer expectations, and in turn, given Dealers much more leverage in dealing with manufacturers.

Another important factor in giving Dealers more independent control than typical franchises is that the automobile dealership is the most capital-intensive franchise business in terms of land, facility, equipment, and inventory cost. Few people can meet the high net-worth requirements.

Another factor in Dealer-factory tension is customer satisfaction. Over time and numerous business-economic cycles, Dealers have come to feel as though the factory's perception of the customer shifts with the economy and sales volumes. (This is a result of changing factory emphasis on the importance of CSi vs. warranty cost controls with shifting sales revenues. When sales were strong, support for the customer was high. When sales dropped, emphasis quickly shifted to tight warranty management.) Dealers also tend to feel that wholesale contacts should fix all the dealerships problems as "givens" of the franchise (rather than relying on their own hiring, training, paying, and supporting of top retail managers). This feeling has evolved primarily because of the high investment required. And because of the perceived high value of the franchise, a debate over Dealer vs. Wholesale responsibility has also evolved. As manufacturers have been forced to cut back on in-field support to gain cost-control, Dealers have often felt "undervalued and forgotten."

We've also seen that the automobile business is the single industry most affected by state and federal regulations (safety, emissions, fuel economy, consumer protection, commercial) of any manufacturing industry. This impact has been felt as deeply by the Dealer as by the manufacturer, driving up costs and the degree of business liability to very high levels. Basically, Dealers feel as though they have a high personal financial stake, carry a major part of the manufacturer's image and success, and deserve more attention and consideration—both as a voice in the business and as an independent business—than they receive. They also feel as though they are the front-line market contact, and thus have nearly as much influence on customer purchase decisions as the product does.

Not only is the automobile dealership the most capital-intensive franchise, but the high constant cash flow demand created by inventory financing and warranty management have made it difficult to convince Dealers to spend money on important areas like Customer Assistance Managers, training for their customer contact people, customer satisfaction systems—fixed overhead expenses that require planning, capital investments, and a long-term view and that prize loyalty over short-term income. The Dealer's view, driven by the operating report and cash flow, tends to be very short-term, and understandably so. This makes Dealers quick to fire employes, including managers, and obsessed with cutting **all** non-productive, non-recoverable costs.

Often, Dealer Principals do not stay as personally involved in the day-to-day business to the degree required to recognize and support quality management. This often results in poor general management and a lack of empowerment for the dealership employes. This usually means very high turnover in management and poor consistency in operations or customer service. So, it's important to keep Dealer Principals active in managing the business. And they must be fully trained in every aspect of the Warranty Management System, business planning, customer service focus, operations management, and local marketing. It's also important to convince Dealers to involve their managers in the total management of the dealership. One of the most difficult things for many Dealers, for example, is to share the operating statement with their Sales Manager, and in particular with their Service and Parts Managers, a must for sound management.

Dualing Practice

The practice of "dualing" is another unique aspect of the auto business. Dealers will want to dual as many brands and product lines as they feel are necessary to fill the market in their area of influence. This business feature was what originally gave the Japanese their entry to U.S. markets. Conversely, Dealers are **very** sensitive about their manufacturer's placement of "competitors" in their marketing area. (Saturn's "Market Area Approach" process may be seen as a viable solution to this long-standing problem.) These things often increase the "business tension" between Dealer and manufacturer. As a result, manufacturers have to compete for "shelf-space" (resources and selling attention by the Dealer) in dealerships with the other product-lines of their dualed Dealers; this also impacts the Dealer's display and facility design requirements, making it tough for the manufacturer to maintain consistent brand image. (The whole issue of "exclusivity" in facility, signage and other areas is becoming a key competitive issue, as manufacturers press Dealers to recapture lost image and brand equity.) Often, each line a Dealer carries has its own standards, operating agreement requirements, reporting requirements, etc. Dealers often feel they are put to unnecessary expense to meet multiple manufacturers' requirements—especially when many of those requirements are redundant and don't offer any "value-added" to the franchise.

The "business management point" product line in a dual dealership has both advantages and disadvantages. (This designates which division, in a dual dealership, is responsible for primary Sales and

Service Agreement administration and franchising management.) While they are closer to the Dealer's operations, through managing the operating report, they still have to compete for shelf-space, advertising, training, and parts, especially with foreign or non-GM duals. And, while they must supply more wholesale support, they may have no more influence than other product lines. Today, it is becoming increasingly important for a division/brand to rely on the value of the consultation and business support they give a Dealer, rather than traditional "business management point," to earn a Dealer's attention and appropriate resources dedicated to brand sales and service.

Multiple sales-forecasting (both vehicles and parts forecasts) requirements in a multi-line dealership make it difficult for the factory to drive the Dealers desired inventory **vs.** required (by the agreement) inventory. Unless the Dealer has an excellent business plan, and thoroughly understands his market, it is very difficult to find the right mix of products across several vehicle lines—especially when the divisions and other manufacturers represented by the Dealer have products that overlap the same market segments. A future key to success in the industry is the move from traditional "push" to "pull" marketing, with product distribution driven from the marketplace by the customer. For this transition to work, Dealers will have to become consistently accurate forecasters. This will be one of the most important functions of the Dealer Business Planning process.

The Dealer As An Independent Business Person

Historically, the automotive Dealer has had tremendous latitude as an independent business person—more so than any other franchise type. Most state laws reflect this. This limits what business, financial, and policy requirements the manufacturer can require the Dealer to comply with. The independent status of the auto Dealer was established primarily by the senate hearings that took place under the Eisenhower administration in 1956. These proceedings, which came to be known as the "Dealers' Day-In-Court" Act, charged the manufacturers with heavy-handed tactics in the franchising process.

Specifically, Dealers accused the manufacturers of undue pressure to "pull" the franchise (which was then open to annual renewal) if sales volumes targets were not made, of requiring the Dealer to carry and pay for "unsaleable inventory overstocks," and of price-fixing tactics (related to the Donaldson Brown Fixed Volume Formula). The Dealers won the litigation, and as a result, established their unique strength as independent business operators. This confrontation reinforced the adversarial relationship between factory and Dealer.

As the result of the 1956 "Dealers' Day in Court" and of supporting states' legislation, Dealers' marketing and business planning is less controlled by the manufacturer than in any other franchise business. (Example: The level of McDonald's daily control over inventory, reporting, and standards could not be enforced in the auto industry.) This is a result of many other factors beyond the act: reaction to Ford's early heavy-handed control, the high level of personal involvement and investment required of Dealers, multi-line competition, the pressure for protected market areas, and the anti-trust fears of the 50s and 60s. This means that the factory must often lead by demonstrated competence rather than by edict.

The sales forecasting process in the auto industry has become, over time, a negotiation, with Wholesale's objective being to maintain their manufacturer's target line-rates at assembly plants, and the Dealers' objective being to target as much **desirable** inventory as possible. (The key is inventory mix, with Dealers wanting hot sellers and factory "trading" slow sellers.)

Running an auto dealership requires, without question, the highest level and broadest range of sales, technical and business skills of any manufacturing-based franchise business. This created the need for intense, continuous training to support rapidly developing technologies. Training the automotive Dealer is a far more complex issue than any other franchise, involving product, Sales and Service, Operations, Management, Business Planning, Customer Satisfaction, and other issues. Historically, Dealers have often felt that this training has been inconsistent, redundant, and poorly coordinated with product and policy.

The manufacturer's Wholesale field organization has come to use vehicle distribution as a tool to leverage Dealers into doing what the manufacturer wants, putting much strain on the business partnership.

This situation, along with the demand for customer satisfaction, has brought about the need for accurate, shared business planning and for developing shared business goals.

Customer Satisfaction

Customer satisfaction is an excellent example of a positive, valuable goal becoming a point of continuing conflict between manufacturer and Dealer. It is a strategy clearly meant to improve sales, but that became something else—a point of leverage in controlling Dealer operations. The Customer Satisfaction Index or CSi, as it was conceived, was meant to be a diagnostic tool, but in some cases Dealers felt it had come to be used as another means of leverage, with Dealers attempting to "buy" votes from customers and the factory using results as a means of punishment and reward through manufacturer recognition programs. The tension escalated to the point that many Dealers came to view CSi as a manufacturer's ploy to gain direct control over "pulling the franchise." The growth of third party reviewers, like J.D. Power, has now moved customer satisfaction from a business design objective to a marketing game-board with successful manufacturers showcasing and advertising high ratings.

One of the most important (and difficult) demands placed on the automotive Dealer has been the requirement to reach a "perfect balance" between warranty management and customer satisfaction. Dealers have long felt pressure to control the warranty-cost-per-vehicle they generate, keeping it in-line with zone and national manufacturers' averages. At the same time, they have faced growing pressure (especially intense since the late 1970s) to maintain a high CSi. There has been a persistent feeling among Dealers that these are conflicting objectives; that forcibly lowering the amount of warranty spent per customer would also lower customer satisfaction. This feeling was especially strong before the late 1980s. Since this time, vehicle quality has risen so significantly that warranty expense has automatically been driven down, and customer satisfaction has risen in proportion. The answer to this dilemma then has become: high vehicle quality, well-trained technicians, skilled retail warranty managers, prompt factory reimbursement, and (perhaps most important) shared retail/wholesale objectives to manage warranty **and** satisfy customers as complementary, not conflicting, goals.

On the other side of the coin, the retail network has evolved the Dealer Satisfaction Index or DSi as a means of rewarding/punishing the manufacturer, the Dealer's answer to the manufacturers' CSi. And like CSi, achieving a high DSi is primarily a function of **shared business goals** between Dealer and manufacturer.

The National Automobile Dealers' Association (NADA) and Dealer Councils have grown into guardians of Dealers' perspective, often working as "war councils" with manufacturers. (Hopefully, with the Saturn and Oldsmobile Board of Governance process, that has retailers actively sharing in **all** areas of product and policy decision-making, this relationship will begin to shift to a real business partnership with common objectives and strategies.)

Chapter 2

The Manufacturer-Dealer Relationship

In a business so crucially interdependent, logic says there should be strong cooperation between manufacturer and distributor. Unfortunately, what should be a strong business partnership with common objectives has in many areas become adversarial. Many issues are involved. In the last chapter we examined some of these issues. Others include: lack of Dealer input into products, policies, distribution patterns vs. real market demands, consistent forecasting methods, lack of a common planning process, and a basic distrust that shows up in areas like warranty.

Currently, one of the most sensitive areas to the Dealer is the cost-to-retail a new unit. This has grown, over time, with labor costs, materials costs, factory programs, and sensitivity to the economy, to the point that it has reached the $1,500 - $1,600 per unit level in the early 1990s. Advertising expense, retail sales compensation, and floor plan interest accounts for about $1,000 of this cost. Sales department assessed rent, utilities, employe Social Security, benefits, and training account for $500 to $600. The manufacturer controls a number of elements that contribute to these costs, including manufacturing labor costs, advertising assessments, Dealer Communications System (DCS) costs, sales promotions, special tools, displays, and training assessments. Another cost factor is interest rates, which due to low inflation, currently save the average Dealer about $150 per unit. Add to this the fact that the average Dealer today retails about 550 units, yet these costs require a volume nearer 750 units to maintain profitability, and you have the basis for one of the industry's greatest challenges: **profitable market-share**, in which the manufacturer's and Dealer's goals are **both** met, with the manufacturer raising its share of the market at the same time **both** Dealer and manufacturer profit grows.

Product—Dealer Lack of Interaction

Historically, Dealers have seen new car and truck products only after designs are locked in, typically at ride-and-drives. The Dealers, the resource that deals daily with the customer, have not had the chance to offer their first-hand input. Dealers represent an excellent source about what is acceptable and what is not to the customer, on everything from pricing, design, option packaging, to service features. What Dealers need are tools to help them measure customer reaction, and training in assessing and using the voice of the customer to improve their customer support performance.

Delivery time (necessary for the factory to fill a customer's order) has been another sore point with Dealers and customers. The pressure is on to sell from Dealer stock rather than delivering what the customer wants through the ordering process. (This leads into what may become one of the main competitive differentiators for the industry in the next decade—mass customization that includes order-to-delivery times of one week or less!)

Another product-related area of concern to Dealers is the parts business. Specifically, this means the cost of parts, the difficulty in getting parts, the difficulty in maintaining a well-balanced parts inventory, and the types of parts promotions that provide price breaks to Dealers on low-need components, but often not on critical parts. This is an example of vertically integrating parts operations into the manufacturing structure, and on making the parts manufacturer's top priority profit rather than customer satisfaction. In this context, manufacturing parts and service parts often "do battle" in supplying new vehicles on the assembly line vs. the dealership. And Dealers are often forced to pay premiums and wait extended times for high-need parts for "down" vehicles.

Field fixes for known problems on vehicles are another area of Dealer concern. Manufacturer's Technical Assistance Center (TAC) operations, Field Engineering Operations, etc., have grown in response to this situation. The difficulty has been the long time required to bring about design and manufacturing changes in vehicles, once problems are identified.

The length of time required to design and produce new and replacement products is a long-standing point of friction with Dealers. The new product design cycle, traditionally a five to seven year process, has now been reduced to as low as 30 months by Chrysler and Toyota. While this has required a massive redo in strategy, it is still far longer than Dealers would like to see. (This is a high priority area for customers as well.)

Related to this is the long time required to get delivery on an ordered vehicle, a problem that often drives customers from one Dealer to another (and from one manufacturer to another). This, of course, is also the major reason Dealers sell from stock and why 45-60 day inventories are necessary to serve the average, urban Dealer's market.

Financial Concerns

Rebates, a phenomenon of the past 12 to 15 years in the industry, have become a concern for Dealers who fear that this reaction to intense competition and overproduction of certain models has become a way of life in the business. This outcome of overcapacity and too many models in too few markets will be a difficult feature of the business to change.

In general, pricing is another critical issue to Dealers, who feel that there is poor productivity and cost-management on the part of the manufacturer (and on the part of unions). GM has the highest cost-per-unit of any manufacturer (although major improvement is now being made in this area). The result, Dealers feel, has been to limit their profit margin. (In Saturn, there's now an attempt to make the three players—manufacturer, Dealer, plant worker—all part of the strategy picture as a way of gaining better control of cost-per-unit). Parts pricing, too, is another long-standing concern. Typically, a manufacturer's in-house parts are far more expensive than their aftermarket equivalents.

The speed of warranty response (which has improved greatly in the past five years) has historically been a financial concern for the Dealer. Today, while delays are often the result of poor management or improper Dealer procedures, it still retains a shadow effect. This is vitally important, since Dealers typically pay much of their fixed operating expenses out of warranty reimbursement. One of the keys to improvement in this area is convincing the Dealer to hire and compensate quality warranty and business managers instead of relying on lower paid "claims clerks." Poorly prepared documentation not submitted in a timely fashion is, by far, the greatest cause of delays in warranty reimbursements.

Price points on competitive, high-profile product lines are a major point of contention in an industry that lives and dies on productivity and other features of cost management. A good example is the Chrysler L-H product, which has established a new level of quality, style and performance in full-sized family sedans for a base price under $18,000.

As a small, independent businessperson, program prices from the franchisor—for merchandising, training, parts, etc.—are always of great concern to the Dealer. So it's absolutely vital that the manufacturer be able to deliver **and** demonstrate real value in the things he asks a Dealer to fund though his open parts account. Executed properly, these business, communication, and technical training programs can form one of the most positive aspects of the franchise.

Recognition of Dealers

One of the most important functions a manufacturer performs is recognizing Dealers for their performance. All small businessmen are competitive, so the recognition process is a most important one. And ego is a hallmark of the successful Dealer. Therefore, it's important to the manufacturer that criteria for recognition accurately represent the performance that is important to Dealer and manufacturer success. Customer satisfaction, sales volume, training, compliance with warranty and policy guidelines, program implementation (like standards systems), are all mutually beneficial to the Dealer and the manufacturer, and therefore the most important measures of success for recognition.

Perhaps the most beneficial (and important) way to recognize Dealers is through their involvement in the business decision-making process. Traditional Dealer Councils began in an attempt to do this. However, they soon became highly politicized forums in which "factory-friendly" Dealers traded "to do" lists with manufacturers, and little real change was generated.

Over the past few years, particularly with the Saturn and Oldsmobile Boards of Governance and GMC Trucks revised Dealer Council process, this situation has taken a dramatic turn for the better, and Dealers, for the first time, are becoming true business partners. (In the Saturn format, Dealers are given a "UAW Partner" to call in Spring Hill.) Not coincidentally, the UAW's participation in the process has been another change for the better, giving the factory worker and Dealer empathy for one another. Today, all GM Divisions are making dramatic improvements in the manufacturer-Dealer partnership through refining their Dealer Councils into true, strategic, shared-planning bodies.

Management Assistance

In any franchise-based industry, the three most important values of the franchise are the product, marketing assistance for selling the product, and the business management know-how of the franchisor. Historically, automobile franchises have been great perceived-value businesses. Dealers have an opportunity to be among the highest paid executives in American industry. Since the business has become so competitive since the late 1970s, however, the importance of the three factors has grown, and the Dealer's satisfaction with them has lessened.

Now, when the Dealer's need for management input has become so important, the manufacturer's ability to implement it has reached an all-time low. This is because of the need for efficiency and cost-cutting, which has taken a great toll on the manufacturer's sales and service field organization, particularly among some of the most experienced people. So the Dealer is more sensitive than ever before in the history of the business about the difficulty of getting a quick, knowledgeable response from the manufacturer.

In line with these concerns, the Dealer expects the manufacturer to help solve all of his customers' problems (since they involve the manufacturer's products and policies), while the manufacturer wants the Dealer to be the main source of problem resolution (since he is the first-line contact and image source). This is another point of entrepreneurial contention that must be solved.

Another important concern in the area of consulting assistance involves convincing the Dealer to employ key individuals, including Warranty Administrators, Customer Assistance Managers, and Training Managers, who will serve as advocates of the business, the customer, and the Dealership employe respectively. Each of these positions involves a long-term investment, primarily aimed at building customer loyalty and other long-term gains. As such, these personnel may be difficult to fund in the short-term, and given the constant cash flow requirement of the retailer, they're "tough sells" for the manufacturer to make. It is absolutely vital that the Dealer understand their importance and get as much help as possible from the manufacturer, through lowered transaction costs, to make them affordable. Dealers must understand that it's not only direct-production, chargeable labor like Technicians and Sales Consultants who are important to the business, but also functions that help the Dealer to build long-term success. Dealers, like all business people, will cut non-direct productive costs when times are difficult and revenue is lowered. The foresight to acquire and retain the type of people and systems that will promote customer loyalty requires a long-term view.

One of the most important "reengineering" changes the automotive manufacturers will have to make to improve efficiency, competitive position and profitability in this decade involves the Wholesale Dealer contact job. This role must become a higher level management position, manned by more experienced people. The position must be fully empowered to make decisions regarding product allocation, franchise placement, warranty and policy than is typical of the business today. The three to four management layers—Regional Managers, Zone Managers and Assistant Zone Managers—that separate the Dealer contact from the factory home office will have to be eliminated. In short, the Dealer contact job will have to become a senior management "Field Executive," a position that top performers with 10 years of service will aspire to, rather than the entry-level job it has been traditionally. Saturn has shown great leadership in this absolutely critical area.

The Long-Term View

One of the most difficult things for a Dealer to cultivate is a long-term "strategic" view of the business—in which owner retention, facility improvement, employe benefit programs, and market knowledge become the management's greatest concerns. This is due to the terrific day-to-day pressure on the Dealer to create and maintain cash flow, just as in any small business that requires high fixed and inventory-maintenance costs.

Another problem is the small businessperson's fixation on short-term results and profit. This again requires maintaining the absolute lowest overhead and inventory, and the highest sales levels. This means a real reluctance to do many of the things required to optimize customer convenience and satisfaction. In the automotive business, unfortunately, the short-term fixation on sales volume, and the measures that reinforce this, prevent Dealers from developing the long-term view of the customer that manufacturers support. Changing this will require fundamental changes in how the business is conducted. For example, some changes are: achieving far higher levels of productivity and quality with resultant price controls, highly automated administration, more precise and lower cost marketing, greater investment in marketing and product design, improvement of the turn-and-earn process with longer-term planning, and conditioning shareholders toward greater reinvestment and focus on capital gain over income. And of course, lowering the cost-to-retail a unit to the Dealer by ferreting out non-value added costs is a top priority for the manufacturer in this area.

Perhaps most important, the Dealer needs to develop a sense of true business partnership with the manufacturer. Dealers must share a common sense of long-term mission and goals with the manufacturer, goals that are built on owner loyalty and on profitable marketshare that satisfies the business and income needs of both parties.

Chapter 3

Profile of a Successful Dealer

We have noted that the job of a retail automotive Dealer is a unique and demanding one. It's no surprise, then, that the person who succeeds in this job will be a unique and special personality. The more the manufacturer (particularly wholesale and customer assistance people) understands about the Dealer's mindset, priorities, requirements and professional style, the more successful the business partnership will be. With this goal—the most positive retail-wholesale relationship possible—in mind, let's build a composite profile of the successful automotive Dealer. (The pronoun "he" is used to simplify the text, but the reader should be aware that more and more successful women Dealers are emerging in the auto business today.)

The successful Dealer:

- **Has a history of success.** He has a track record of business success, both inside and outside the automotive industry. He has also built and/or run profitable companies and is a proven businessperson.

- **Has had experience in small businesses.** Very few are from "Fortune 100" positions. Most would not be comfortable in a middle-management role in a large company. The typical successful small business person, particularly Dealers, like fast, flexible organizations that **they** control. Dealers are entrepreneurs that want to start, own and run their own business.

- **Has an entrepreneurial mentality and is an innovator**, not a "continuous improver." He focuses on "breakthroughs" over incremental change.

- **Is well capitalized** and usually has a high net-worth. He has access to financing and credibility as a credit risk, as well as having accumulated a strong investment portfolio.

- **Possesses strong leadership traits**, sales skills, has a high "E" Factor (ego, extrovert), and is charismatic, open and an appealing communicator.

- **Has a very big ego.** He enjoys being "center stage" and needs continuous reinforcement and acknowledgement. He may tend to the "flashy" in dress and personal style and want to be first, best, right, and visible. This person is not afraid to "have the ball at crunch time."

- **Trusts his own judgement**; tends to be visionary and is not afraid of risk **if** he can control the variables. This person is a leader, **not** a follower. In addition, he can be argumentative and confrontational in approach and have a high level of "street sense" (intuitive, perceptive).

- **Is usually self-focused**; he keeps his own counsel and makes his own decisions based on his belief in himself. Yet he tends to be very sensitive to criticism, real or perceived.

- Loves making **"The Deal;"** The leader in this profile is a strong negotiator and a creative "packager." He presents a position in the most creative and advantageous light. This leader is always looking for opportunities and in taking advantage of opportunities, will often overextend himself at a **very** high energy level. He tends to have a short-term focus. He also has an aversion to "one-price," exclusivity concepts; he wants full freedom to develop a wide-open deal.

- **Loves to win** and is **highly** competitive. He always wants to lead peers and loves being the first to accomplish any goal.

- **Distrusts outside authority.** This trait excludes being suspicious of "control." He is the antithesis of the "corporate executive" and favors the "simple" over the complex.

- **Does well under pressure.** He thrives on confrontation and opposition and often carries the organization in down-cycles.

- **Needs recognition—personal and professional.** Our Dealer is motivated by the need for recognition and positive visibility. He wants to "set the standard."

Chapter 4

The Healthy Dealer

Dealer Needs

To become and remain profitable and successful, a Dealer depends on certain critical factors. A successful retail operation needs:

- **Cash flow** to meet fixed and semi-fixed, general and administrative expenses, payroll and benefits, rent, utilities, phones, facility maintenance, etc.

- **Service and Parts fixed operations** that provide the basic source of meeting expenses required to operate the business, that is, the fixed overhead costs. In a strong dealership, the Service Department covers 100% and more of the business' fixed overhead. And, strong fixed operations are the Dealer's key to getting through economic downturns (when new vehicle sales drop) with their business intact and even profitable in spite of lower vehicle sales volume.

- **Warranty work**, which is an absolutely vital element of the dealership's cash flow. Service repair work needed by the dealership's customers during the warranty period is an important part of cash flow that the Dealer strongly relies on.

- **A precise balance between effective warranty management and optimum customer satisfaction.** This is the basic pressure in the retail business. And it characterizes all good, profitable, and long-term successful Dealers, Dealers who consistently satisfy their customers, manage their warranty business, generate minimal comebacks, retain their customers for the full ownership cycle, and then resell to a loyal owner base.

- **Consistent instructions regarding Warranty Management and Customer Satisfaction**—particularly in difficult economic times when sales are down. In these times, Dealers feel they must both limit warranty expense and improve customer satisfaction. But the best Dealers understand that they must have **both** sound warranty and satisfied customers, and that the two should be complementary and not "mutually exclusive."

- **Wholesale Support**—another irony of the retail business revolves around wholesale support for the Dealer. In difficult economic times, when profits are squeezed at every level, manufacturers often cut back on experienced field staff, at a time when Dealers are in greatest need of administrative support and experienced consultation. Unfortunately, this is often another example of cutting back on short-term "nonproductive" expenses that can endanger long-term business growth. The manufacturer must have the most experienced and skilled managers **at the retail interface**, particularly in difficult times. Conversely, when revenues are squeezed, Dealers will often take parallel, short-sighted expense control measures that put them in the most jeopardy. They may focus on less training, eliminating customer contact personnel, cutting advertising, "shortcutting" first-rate new vehicle delivery, cutting back on good parts inventories—all functions which directly hurt technical performance and customer service. Good Dealers concentrate on maintaining the things that can generate the most revenue when unit sales dip in a weak economy.

- **Effective Warranty Administration.** A common problem occurs when a Dealer either eliminates a good claims clerk, or won't spend what is required to keep a qualified warranty manager—relying on the factory wholesale person to process dealership warranty. In this situation a Dealer often loses the "feel" for the state of his customers and his business.

- **Information**—about product problems, fixes, warranty, etc. Dealers often feel they are the "last to know." Good retail communications are an absolute must for a Dealer's success.

- **Ethical Dealing.** Reluctant to lose any deal, a retail salesperson will often get a customer into an "upside-down" deal by inflating trade-in values and financing an amount that prevents the customer from ever having more equity in the vehicle than the outstanding loan during the life of the contract. This gets at the very core of ethical business practices which, in the past, have given the business a negative image. Changing this situation is one of the most important steps in building the customer's trust in the manufacturer and the Dealer.

- **Expense Management.** Many times, the Dealer puts himself into a difficult cash position by poorly managing expenses, thus creating "leaks" that hurt his operating position. An example of this is poor follow-up on overdue receivables. A good retail business manager (an absolute must for any successful dealership) pays close attention to expense management, keeping receivables current, and balancing cash flow with payables.

- **Staffing Plans.** The successful Dealer recruits talented technicians, salespersons, managers, etc.; without doubt this is one of the most important tasks a Dealer must do. This becomes very difficult for a number of reasons—the need for competitive salaries, a clear understanding of career path, a benefits program etc., all of which impact loyalty to the dealership.

Good Dealers offer all these things and concentrate on building "employe enthusiasm." A good Dealer also maintains detailed job descriptions for each position, and uses them as training guides and performance review outlines. The successful Dealer hires and develops top-performing managers and works with them on a regular basis to keep abreast of all the business operations ratios that measure the health of the business i.e.,—CSi, profitability, investment in advertising and training, warranty management, etc.

- **Principal Involvement.** The good Dealer keeps **objective** track of the performance of his people and his business. So keeping the Dealer Principal involved in the day-to-day operation of the business is an important objective, along with ensuring that the retail management team is well trained and consists of the best possible performers. The good Dealer can be found in the dealership actively involved with day-to-day management of the business. He knows his employes and understands their strengths and weaknesses.

- **Inventory Mix.** The Dealer's inventory mix **must** represent the demands of the local market. This is one of the most important elements of a good Dealer Business Plan. The Dealer often does a poor job of setting up and maintaining an effective product and parts inventory, in both cases hurting customer convenience and satisfaction. Understanding how to do an accurate units and parts sales forecast is the first step in a successful Dealer business plan.

- **Facility.** A facility that promotes customer convenience; Ample, marked parking, lounge areas, signage location, furniture, decor, entertainment devices, are all part of this.

- **Line of Credit.** A commercial line-of-credit that exceeds 90 days of the average monthly expenses, including fixed and variable expenses, is very important. The Dealer also needs a strong capital base, which should be greater than the GM requirement.

- **A strong merchandising and advertising program.** This includes participation in an ad association and a strategy that makes use of all local media. It also requires a strong seasonally-based service and parts merchandising program.

- **Competitive products.** These must meet local market and customer requirements, be superior to competition, priced properly, and be supported by a strong financing program.

- **Positive Dealer/Manufacturer Partnership.** The Dealer must view the manufacturer as a real business partner. At times, in an effort to retain the customer, the Dealer will cast the manufacturer as the "bad guy"—placing the burden for a product problem, out of warranty condition, policy decision, etc.—with the factory. This is another example of a poor business partnership that must be changed. It also is a sign of poor retail-wholesale communications.

The bottom-line is that running a dealership through all types of economic cycles is a difficult and complex challenge requiring talented management, customer focus, a well trained and compensated work force, and most importantly, cash flow that consistently exceeds expenses.

Signs of a Healthy Dealer From the Marketing Division's Perspective

The "big picture" view of the overall business health of a Dealer is based on the combination of the Dealer's operations (sales, revenues, profitability), performance and the long-term objectives and strategies of the manufacturer, in this case the GM Marketing Division.

Along with its specific brand-image based strategies, the Division has three basic long-term objectives:

1. Market-Share Improvement
2. Customer Satisfaction Improvement
3. Dealer Satisfaction Improvement.

To achieve these objectives, the Marketing Division needs these key long-term strategies:

- Strengthen the Dealer organization
- Increase market-share, **profitably**
- Deliver the best overall ownership experience of any manufacturer.

For the individual Dealer to contribute to achieving these objectives, he must fully understand certain information about the business in order to make quality business decisions. This understanding begins with the Dealer providing answers to these basic questions:

- Who are **my** competitors (specific other dealerships in the Dealer's local market), and how do I compare to them?

- What are the external (marketplace) threats to my business—from competition, economic conditions, local business situation and local demographics?

- What are my internal (dealership) strengths and weaknesses— as related to the competition and market situation?

- How do these things translate into viable opportunities for my dealership?

Knowing the right answers to these questions is the key for wise allocation of the Dealer's resources—capital, manpower, facilities, and tools and equipment. Knowing the answers **and** using this knowledge in managing their resources efficiently, greatly improve the Dealer's ability to react quickly to shifting market conditions.

The first step for the Divisional Wholesale contact person in understanding any Dealer's performance is to take a step back and ask these three questions:

1. Is the Dealer selling product? (based on reasonable Dealer forecast vs. actual sales)

2. Is the Dealer making money?

3. Is the Dealer satisfying customers? (as shown by CSi and retained owner loyalty)

To answer these questions, the contact person needs to investigate the Dealer's performance in seven areas:

1. Vehicle Registration Analysis and Performance to Forecast
2. Sales Management
3. Customer Satisfaction
4. Fixed Operations (Service and Parts)
5. Financial Analysis
6. Training and Personnel
7. Facilities.

The vehicle information database, customer, and Dealer histories used by each General Motors Division contains a number of performance indicators to facilitate analyzing these seven areas. The balance of this chapter examines these seven areas, explains the purpose of the dealership review, and suggests things to look for in each area.

1. **Vehicle Registration Analysis and Sales Performance vs. Forecast.**

a. The first step in this analysis is to review the **Dealer's actual sales performance vs. the Dealer's sales forecast**. A good Dealer sales forecast, a key element in the Dealer Business Plan, is the basis for forecasting the Dealer's cash flow, gross profit and variable profit for the dealership. Each GM car and truck Division should use their particular Dealer forecast information. These systems provide Unit Sales Forecasts compared to Actual Unit Deliveries for each current six-month period. Variation between actual and forecast provides a basis for determining if forecasts are too aggressive or too conservative, if inventories are correct to support forecast, if markets or competitors have been correctly evaluated, and what types of changes must be made to correct the situation.

b. The next step in this evaluation requires a review of **the Dealer's Market Segmentation**. This review will help to determine how important each vehicle segment is in a given market. The basic resource for this review is the "Sales and Registration Report" that each Division has available in its databases. This report normally provides: Retail Registrations in the Dealer's APR (Area of Primary Selling Responsibility), Dealer's Retail Sales, and Fleet Registrations in the Dealer's APR. These reports will provide each market segment's contribution to the total vehicle industry in the Dealer's APR (or Area of General Sales and Service Agreement for Multiple Dealer Areas). It also allows comparison of the Dealer's performance to the Division's national average for each segment, revealing areas of potential opportunity.

c. **Review of Lost Sales** is the third step. Lost Sales represent a weakness in the Dealer's coverage of the market, which translates directly into lost profits for the Dealer. Lost Sales can be evaluated by looking at Sales Information, Registration History, and Registration Effectiveness Reports in the sales history database system. The Sales Information makes it possible to analyze how the Dealer's market-share compares to averages for the particular Division's District, Zone, Area, and National areas. If the Dealer's share runs below these, Lost Sales are calculated based on registration data for the current year. Lost Sales can then be translated from registrations to deliveries using the delivery data available in the Vehicle Registration History. If there are consistently more deliveries reported than registrations, the dealership is "pumping out" vehicles and Lost Sales may be overstated. If there are fewer deliveries than registrations, other dealerships are "pumping in" vehicles and the Lost Sales are understated. It's important to understand exactly how actual deliveries measure up to comparable Dealer market-share performance, and the registrations **vs.** deliveries balance to see just how well the Dealer is doing within his assigned market.

d. The final area to review in Sales **vs.** Forecast is **Fleet and Commercial Sales Opportunities.** Fleet and Commercial Sales represent a significant profit opportunity for many Dealers. Getting the Dealer to **commit** to the commercial business is the key. Car and truck Divisions have their own commercial reports. These reports provide Retail Registrations in the Dealer's APR, Dealer Retail Sales, and Fleet Registrations in the Dealer's APR. Using these reports, the wholesale contact person can determine what the total size and makeup of the fleet market is in a Dealer's APR. From this information, the wholesale contact person should assemble a proposal that details commercial fleet sales projections, contract maintenance for servicing these sales, parts inventories to service the sales, and finance and insurance potentials to cover the sales. Contract maintenance for commercial fleets is an outstanding business opportunity that Dealers often miss. It's very important that they understand the **total** potential in fleet/commercial sales, vehicles **and** parts and service.

2. Sales Management.

a. **Inventory vs. Sales Forecast.** The ability of a dealership to meet its sales forecast depends on having the right products to meet specific customer needs in the Dealer's market. To determine inventory requirements, the sales forecast should be used rather than day's supply, since the forecast is based on

anticipated rather than past sales. (However, it's a good idea to **compare** the two to determine how well the Dealer's doing vs. potential.) The appropriate database, which will contain the sales forecast (from the Business Plan), inventory, delivery, and days supply for each Dealer, should be used. In most cases, this information will provide a six-month, by-vehicle analysis of unit-sales forecasts vs. actual unit deliveries. As a rule of thumb, the dealership should have at least 90 days of future sales on-the-ground, in-transit, and in-system. And of course, the sales forecast data is the basis for establishing parts inventories so that four or more inventory turns per year can be realized. (Four turns is a healthy business goal. The Dealer should be satisfied with no less than three parts inventory turnovers per year.)

b. **Order Bank Requirements.** Once the inventory requirements vs. forecast have been determined, the next step is to translate those requirements into orders. To do this, the wholesale contact person should look at the activity summary in the sales database, vehicle orders on-hand, in-system and inventory listing. The Sales Order Bank should be detailed, using the Dealer's inventory requirements and by-vehicle forecasts.

c. **Order Bank Management.** The above process for Order Bank requirements to meet forecasts should be recalculated each month to assure that the dealership has a proper mix of inventory, sufficient for the Dealer's sales rate and market preferences by model. Remember, good forecasts go beyond the number of units sold and identify the specific make-up of projected sales by vehicle models.

d. **Delivery Listing.** Proper and timely delivery reporting by a Dealer is critical for the Dealer's ability to earn future product on the turn-and-earn system supported by the business plan. In the future, if true "pull-marketing" is achieved, the plan forecasts will drive allocation. For the time being, however, the company still uses the traditional system that drives distribution based on the Dealer's past performance in each vehicle line and model. The two tools the contact person should use to accomplish this are the "Days to Report

Deliveries" monthly report and the Dealer's inventory listing in the sales databases. These will document average days between vehicle delivery and entry into the Dealer Communications System and inventory details including invoice date and total days in inventory.

e. **Advertising and Promotions.** The purpose of this is for the wholesale contact person to be sure that the Dealer is featuring the Division's products in its advertising strategy. This is especially critical when the Dealer is a dual. The objective of a good advertising strategy is to provide a continuous awareness and new products program that will attract buyers, help create a desirable dealership image, create showroom traffic and stay within a realistic budget. The Dealer should use a mix of media—newspaper, radio, local TV, and direct mail—based on market demographics (incomes, buying patterns, geography, etc.). And of course, it's important to ensure a Dealer is active in the local retail ad association.

f. **Dedicated Division-Product Resources.** Selling and servicing each Division's trucks and cars is a unique part of the automotive business, and has special requirements. The Dealer must make sure that the proper amount of capital, manpower, and equipment is dedicated to each line of business. And, when cars and trucks are sold, the dealership must evaluate the need for (in addition to its car-oriented managers) a New Truck Sales Manager, trained truck salespersons, truck displays, truck parts inventory, identification program, and truck-specific meetings and training sessions, in addition to their passenger car counterparts. Again, one of wholesale's most important responsibilities is to ensure that sales and service of their Division's product and image treatment receive a full complement of dealership resources in the dualed dealership.

g. **Sales Transportation Consultation Training.** It is also **very** important for passenger car and truck retail sales people to be trained in the specific techniques of transportation counseling required by their Divisions. This will ensure that the retail sales process is centered on the **customer's** specific transportation needs, matching ideal vehicle(s) to these needs, an absolute must in customer satisfaction.

3. **Customer Satisfaction.**

a. **CSi Performance to Forecast.** All Dealers developing Business Plans are required to set CSi goals for their dealerships. Goals should be set for CSi indexes for Dealer Sales Satisfaction, Warranty Service Satisfaction, and Dealer Overall Satisfaction. Most Division databases provide a current, three-month moving average of these goals vs. actual CSi, and a GM Franchise Comparison to compare Division scores to other GM lines handled by the Dealer, a Key Satisfaction Indices Screen to compare the 12-month score to the three-month score, Sales Staff Index to compare the Sales Staff 12-month to three-month score, Delivery Condition score, and Warranty Service Details to review fixed operations scores. It's very important for the Dealer to be shown how his sales, service business (customer-pay), and owner loyalty correlate to his CSi performance. In this way, he learns the true **business value** of the customer, and that satisfying customers is more than just a good thing to do; it's **good business practice** and an investment in the future through retaining loyal customers.

b. **Vehicle Delivery Programs.** Divisional new-vehicle delivery programs focus on new vehicle delivery and are designed to give buyers extra attention and care to start building loyalty to the Dealer and the brand early in the ownership experience. Results of these surveys must be reviewed regularly. Whatever format the Division uses, it is important to go through a regular trend review process to analyze just how well a Dealer is doing in the delivery process and the early phase of vehicle ownership. This becomes an excellent guide for training and specific wholesale counseling for each Dealer. All studies show that the first 30 to 90 days of the ownership experience make an indelible imprint on the customer in terms of accepting the product and the Dealer. The Division's delivery process and its databases are key tools in making the most of this vital customer-satisfying opportunity.

4. **Fixed Operations.**

a. **Fixed Operations Performance to Forecast.** This determines whether or not the dealership is achieving the goals it has set for Fixed Operations (Service and Parts) improvement. The Divisional marketing database system provides a summary of sales and profits, both goals and actuals, by month, for the Service Mechanical, Body Shop, and the Parts Department. A consistently profitable fixed operations business is the key to meeting the fixed costs of the business, and in tough economic times, it can be **the** key to a successful dealership.

b. **Fixed Coverage Performance to Forecast.** This determines how the dealership is doing toward meeting its goal for Fixed Coverage, i.e., how well the gross profits from the Fixed Operations are covering the total dealership's fixed overhead expenses. The basic goal, of course, is for Service and Parts gross profits to cover 100% of the fixed overhead expenses. Highly efficient Service Operations that do a large volume of customer-pay as well as warranty, working at least 100% capacity in terms of available labor hours, utilizing at least 100% facility/service stall efficiency, and selling a large volume of service, counter, and commercial parts, will commonly cover well **over** 100% of their dealership fixed expense through the fixed operations.

5. **Financial Analysis and Performance to Forecast.**

a. **Financial Forecasts.** This determines whether or not the Dealer is achieving the goals set for capitalization, profitability, and asset management. In other words, does the dealership have sufficient liquid capital to meet investment needs, is it generating consistent profit **throughout** its sales and service operations, and is it properly managing its expenses and receivables (warranty, etc.). It's important to note that Working Capital should meet the GM standard so that the Dealer's ability to meet financial commitments and capitalize on things like growth opportunities is not compromised. Also, if the Net Profit Before Business Taxes is above or below forecast, it must be analyzed to see if sales are too low, or expenses are too high. The FACTS Screens are the tools to use here. Finally, a day's supply of parts that is too high (over 120 days) and that may contain too high a percentage of obsolete or non-refundable parts, is an unnecessary burden. Conversely, too low a supply hurts the ability to respond to customers.

b. **FACTS Information.** The FACTS process (used throughout all GM Divisions) paints a picture of how the Dealer is performing financially, i.e., is the dealership properly capitalized; are the expenses under control; and is the dealership making money. Let's examine what to look for:

— Working Capital as a percent of the GM Standard should be at or near 100%. Working capital is vital when a Dealer needs to make important facility improvements, fund inventory expansions, purchase land or capital equipment necessary to upgrade his total servicing capacity.

— Cash and Contracts as a percent of Average Monthly Expenses should be at about 100%. This means cash flow is meeting or exceeding expenses, and the Dealer will not have to draw on a line of credit to meet fixed expenses.

— Dealership Profit should be positive and near the Retail Business Plan Forecast.

— Debt-to-Equity Ratio should be no greater than four to one. Higher proportions mean debt is getting too far beyond the amount of ownership equity that has been achieved in the business.

— Fixed Coverage should be no less than 60% for a Light-Duty/Passenger Car Dealer. (And the Dealer should strive to gain 100% in a single-line dealership.)

— Past Due Receivables should not be excessive. Generally speaking, anything beyond 90 days must be discounted. (Banks typically will not view over-90-day receivables as assets for advancing a line of credit.)

— New Car and New Truck Days Supply should be between 60 and 90 days. Fewer days supply means the Dealer won't be able to supply normal business, and more means interest expense will become overly expensive, putting a greater burden on profit margins in all departments.

— Parts Days Supply should be between 90 and 120 days (four turns per year is a good goal).

— Average Months Claims vs. Warranty Advance should be about a two to one ratio.

— Factory Receivables should not be excessive. Receivables plus cash should cover at least three months' operating expense, but at least 30% of this should be in cash.

c. **Fixed Coverage and Break Even.** A Fixed Coverage review is intended to determine how well the dealership is covering total fixed overhead expense with its gross profits from Fixed Operations. Break-even analysis is used to determine how many new vehicles must be sold each month for the dealership not to lose money, i.e., to "break-even."

The Dealership Break-Even is the number of vehicles that must be sold so that the **Net Profit** from their sale covers the Fixed Overhead **not** covered by **Gross Profits** from Fixed Operations, i.e., overall income exactly equals expenses. With that in mind, follow this procedure for determining Break-Even. (All items referenced are included in the Dealer Operating Statement.)

How To Determine Break-Even:

1. Find total Dealership Fixed Overhead Expense year-to-date (YTD).
2. Find total Dealership Fixed Operations Gross Profit YTD.
3. Subtract Fixed Gross Profit from Fixed Overhead Expense to get Fixed Net Loss (or Profit).
4. Add Net Additions/Deductions YTD to Fixed Net Loss.
5. Find total Dealership Variable Selling Expense YTD.
6. Find total Dealership Variable Gross Profit YTD.
7. Calculate total Dealership Variable Net Profit by subtracting total Variable Selling Expense from total Variable Gross Profit.
8. Divide total Dealership Variable Net Profit by the number of New Units sold to get Variable Net per New Unit.
9. Calculate Dealership Break-Even by dividing Fixed Net Loss +/- Net Add/Deducts by Variable Net Profit per New Unit. This tells you how many New Vehicles a Dealership must sell YTD before it can begin making money. To get a monthly Break-Even, simply divide the YTD figure by the number of months YTD. The figure should be realistic based on the Dealership's past performance and its market. In other words, a Dealer's break-even units number should be realistic based on normal variations, plus or minus 15%, in forecast sales.

6. **Training and Personnel.**

   a. **Available Retail Training Usage.** This review makes sure that dealership Sales and Service personnel are attending the sales skills, service technical, Service Advisor, and management training offered by the Division and by General Motors Training Centers. These indicators help a Dealer diagnose specific training needs. For example, the CSi Comebacks report points out areas of need for Technician training, just as the Sales Staff Index report points out sales training and customer satisfaction training needs.

b. **Personnel Policies and Procedures.** This review is used to assure that the dealership has policies and procedures in place for personnel management. These policies should support the principles of continuous improvement and participative management. These policies and procedures should provide guidelines and processes for:

- Hiring Practices
- Orientation and Job Skills Training
- Career Development Process and Requirements
- Employment Benefits
- Dealership Policies
- Performance Standards (for facility, tools and equipment, financial management, business practices, productivity and efficiency, as well as personnel performance).
- Compensation
- Performance Evaluation Process.

These areas are absolutely crucial to establish the dealership as a place for outstanding employes to build a long term career relationship. The goal is "retail employe enthusiasm," without which GM will never have customer enthusiasm leadership. For example, one of the policies followed by all successful dealerships is an employe benefits plan that includes medical coverage and features like tuition reimbursement and paid vacations and holidays. A retirement plan, such as a 401K annuity program, is another way a Dealer can retain employes and lower turnover. The bottom line is to make the dealership a **career** and not just a job.

As a result, the dealership can attract and retain the best sales, technical, and business people in the industry.

7. **Facilities.**

a. **Overall Facility Appearance.** This review ensures that dealership facilities are safe, attractive, contribute to productivity and customer satisfaction, and perhaps most important, that they properly represent the brand image of the Division. The interior of the dealership should be an attractive, clean, well organized place for employes and customers to do business. Good housekeeping practices are vital in establishing the level of professional environment that attracts and keeps customers.

Visibility and signage are absolute musts for a successful dealership. Customers must be able to readily see the building and locate parking areas, Service area, Body Shop, and find well-organized vehicle inventory. Inside the building, the cashier, customer lounge, and restrooms should be properly signed. Product and point-of-purchase (POP) literature should be readily accessible. Payment methods should be visible. And in all cases, signage should be positive, informative, and consistent in style and color. Labor rates, hours, courtesy transportation, credit terms, and restricted areas should also be clearly signed.

Display and storage space should be ample, and meet GM Facility Guide requirements. Parking should be well maintained and have stripped lot areas, close to the showroom and Service/Body Shop areas.

And perhaps most important, the dealerships overall appearance—use of color, interior and exterior design, furnishing, lighting, quality of carpeting, signage style and graphics should reflect the Division's brand image standards.

Expansion potential is an important advantage for the dealership facility. As part of the dealership's long-term plan, expansion may be a very important consideration in a growing market area.

Lighting should be sufficient to promote a highly visible sales and service area. Color coordination should be consistent, pleasing, and support the Division's colors and logotype styles and image identification.

General housekeeping concerns should include temperature control, ventilation, plenty of comfortable custom seating, current magazines, TV with VCR, vending machines, landscaping that is well trimmed and attractive, fresh paint, and regular cleaning.

b. **Showroom Display and Vehicle Display.** This review is to ensure that vehicles are properly presented and attractively displayed in the showroom, in drive-by displays, and in the dealership's vehicle storage area. It's also important to keep the vehicles on display clean and accessorized to reflect the tastes of the Dealer's market.

Another important aspect of display is the new vehicle delivery area. The best Dealers have an assigned area where new cars and trucks are "presented" to the new owner. Vehicles that are washed, waxed, properly lit, and carefully presented with a full features operations review are all part of the process. Less successful Dealers hand customers the keys, point them at the lot, and wish them good luck. Top Dealers make delivery an event the customer will remember fondly, a real "happening" that shows the Dealer appreciates the customer's investment and is fully committed to supporting that investment over the complete ownership cycle.

Dealer Priorities—A Wholesale Checklist

Top Dealers always have a set of business priorities that must be met consistently in order to set up and maintain a successful retail operation. This section summarizes the "steps" that should be followed in carrying out these priorities. These steps can be used as a checklist by the wholesale representative in consulting with Dealers, or in reviewing the performance of existing dealerships. These are good reminders of issues that should be accounted for in a retail business plan. This checklist is helpful in regularly scheduled steps for Dealership Consulting, and in analyzing problems in a dealership.

1. **Must Research/Understand the Market:**
   — By Brand, Dealer(s)
   — Sales Activity, Registrations
   — Priority Customer Needs—by Market Segments
   — Important Models, Optioning
   — Cost of Improvements

— "Comp/Shop"—A Process of Reviewing Sales History, Turnover, Penetration, Strengths/Weaknesses of Competitors
— Trends in Marketing; Demographics, Psychographics, Patterns in Products, Services and Sales are Reviewed
— Important Customer Conveniences are Understood
— Business Hours; Community Activities and Priorities
— Commercial **and** Personal Use Opportunities are Identified
— Commercial Parts, Services, Municipal Opportunities
— Customer Perceptions of Competition are Understood.

2. **Develop a Management Team and Core of Key Players (Employe Enthusiasm):**
— General Manager
— Business Manager (finance **and** business judgement)
— Technicians
— Sales People
— Claims Administrator
— Service Advisors
— Customer Assistance Manager (C.A.M.)
— Competitive Total Compensation "Package":
  • Compensation
  • Benefits
  • Education
  • Holidays/Vacations
  • "Perqs"
  • Career Plans.

3. **Ensure Advertising and Merchandising Fits Market Profile:**
— Active in Dealer Association Ad Group
— Align Messages with Expectations
— Customer Focus Groups Held Regularly
— Brand Image of Segments.

4. **Strong Operation/Management Process:**
— Business Plan (Operations, Forecasts, Strategies)
— Negotiate Favorable Line-of-Credit; Equity Leverage
— Demonstrate Operational Focus (Forecasts, Expense Management, Receivable Management, Fixed Overhead vs. Revenues)
— Develop Inventories

- Manage Based on Plan
- Parts—Service, Counter, Commercial; 4+ Parts Inventory Turns; Automate parts; inventory management
- Vehicles—45-60 Days Supply; Appropriate Mix.

5. **Establish Employe Recognition System:**
   — Customer Satisfaction
   — Sales, Profit, CSi, Customer Response Process in-Place
   — Advancing the Strategies of Division, Dealer
   — Meeting Business Plan Goals
   — Employe Recognition is Visible; A Clear Priority
   — Value to Employe is Clear.

6. **Implement a Training Plan for All Employes:**
   — Use CSi; Dealer Surveys
   — Include Everyone
   — Required and Optional Training are Included
   — Specialties, Cross-Train; Plan for Every Job Function
   — Dealer-Facilitated Customer Focus Groups are Conducted
   — Career Plan Process is in-Place
   — Training Plan is Linked to Motivation, Rewards.

7. **Keep Daily/Weekly Track of Revenues and Expenses:**
   — Process Warranty Claims Accurately and Promptly:
     - Hire a Top Administrator
     - Align Warranty Management and Customer Satisfaction
   — Generating Liquidity; Cash Flow is Greater than Payables
   — Interest Costs (Inventory, Systems, Line-of-Credit)
   — Fixed/Variable Costs (Keep Fixed Expenses Low)
   — Again-Receivables Control (Should be Less Than 90 Days)
   — Isolate Expense "Leaks"
   — Productivity (Employes, Facilities, Equipment, Systems) is Tracked
   — "Cracking the Nut" (Target Date for Break-Even)
   — Fixed Overhead Coverage; Control the "Umbrella" of Fixed Costs.

8. **Share Trial Balances with Managers:**
   — Using the Business Plan to Budget Change, Improvement

— Planning Advertising, Merchandising
— Impact on Training, Personnel Management
— Gross Profit-per-Unit Analysis
— Receivables, Aging Tracking and Control
— Department/Overall Profit Contribution
— Revenue Patterns
— Expense Patterns
— Fixed Costs **vs.** Service/Parts Revenues
— Negotiate Line-of-Credit with Favorable Terms
— Resources Allocations
— Managing Productivity, Resources, Expenses as a **Team**.

9. **Carefully Monitor Comebacks:**
— As a Guide to Training
— Parts Inventory Analysis
— Look for Trends to Identify Training and Equipment Needs
— As a Quality Evaluation Management Tool.

10. **Maintain a Strict Ethical Dealing Policy:**
— One-Price Approach is One Way; Value-pricing is Another.
— Competitive New Price, Accurate Used Appraisal
— No Upside-Down Deals
— Transportation Counseling Philosophy (Align Product, Budget, Needs)
— Finance & Insurance, Leasing Guidance for Customer
— Full Disclosure on Cost of Ownership; Warranty Coverage; Customer Responsibility; Maintenance Requirements.

11. **Employ a Customer Response Process:**
— Customer Assistance Manager is Employed and Empowered at Level of Department Managers
— Customer Ombudsman (Empowered) is Employed
— Relationship-Based Process is Used, Based on Proactive Customer Contact
— Tracking—Proactive and Reactive is Used
— Trends in Customer Responses are Charted
— Provide Feedback to All Departments on Customer Inputs
— Customer Input Used to Help Drive Training
— Focus for Customer Enthusiasm

— Dealership Trust and Credibility is a Goal
— Build Customer Relationships
— Target Customer Loyalty and Word-of-Mouth Advertising.

Chapter 5

The Unique Role of the Automotive Dealer in American Business

Let's review the points about Dealers' position and their business that make their role so unique in American business. We've looked at the broad requirements for being a successful Dealer: business skills, high net worth, personal style, entrepreneurial spirit, management and leadership characteristics. And we've seen that the automotive dealership is unique among franchise businesses in terms of the complex array of skills and knowledge that are required in so many areas: sales, business, finance, advertising and merchandising, marketing, strategic planning, customer relations and more.

Running a successful and profitable automobile dealership is one of the toughest challenges in American business, and it can be one of the most satisfying and rewarding.

The following checklist shows why the Dealer's role is so unique. It provides a framework for understanding this remarkable profession.

The Dealer's Role—a Checklist

- Responsible for running the most complex franchise business in America; with responsibility to purchase, manage, and operate.

- Requires the broadest range of skills and experience of any franchise business.

- Opens the Dealer Principal to the greatest exposure to publicity, consumer groups, and litigation.

- Serves personal-use, business, and municipal customers in vehicle sales, parts sales, and contract maintenance.

- Involves financing, leasing, and rental connections to a wide range of public and private institutions.

- Has elements of marketing, manufacturing, and service industries.

- Requires high capitalization and continuous cash flow.

- Works in retailing and wholesaling environments.

- Involves the most complex financing relationship with customers.

- Includes multiple lines of business:

  — Retail Sales
  — Commercial Sales
  — Parts (Internal, Counter, Commercial)
  — Rental and Leasing
  — Finance and Insurance
  — Accessorizing
  — Maintenance, Repair
  — Contract Maintenance
  — Body Shop
  — Fleet Sales.

- Provides many formal/informal links to other business and industries.

- Involves a complex, broad range of warranty fulfillment.

- Requires a wide variance in education and training requirements.

- Involves very complex accounting and business management requirements.

- Demands a high level of Business Strategic Operations Planning.

- Requires owning and maintaining a wide range of systems hardware and software, including their operation and programming.

- Demands the greatest investment in equipment, facility, inventory, and property of any franchise business.

- Must deal with the widest variety of supplier, customer businesses.

- Demands understanding and responding to one of the broadest ranges of customer requirements.

- Products and services support both customers' personal and business needs; Products **must** be operational.

- Needs excellent interpersonal, technical, business, marketing, and management skills.

- Demands the most intense involvement with the franchisor.

- Is the most comprehensive **and** independent business relationship of any franchise.

- Gets into the most involved legal, financial, and business interactions.

- Offers **both** the highest risk/reward.

- Is the most adversarial with, **yet** most dependent on the franchisor.

- Can market a number of competitive product lines; **very** unique in business world.

- Must meet multiple business requirements.

- Demands the most intricate and varied sales, service, advertising, merchandising relationship with franchisor, suppliers, **and** customers.

Section III The Economy

Chapter 1

The Economy and the Car Business

Introduction and Overview

The automobile business is one of the major "drivers" in the economic growth and general health of our country. And the economy, in turn, has a huge impact upon the auto industry. So, for people in the automotive industry who are involved in helping customers and Dealers, a knowledge of the economy, its history and how it works is one of the most powerful tools available. We'll start our investigation of the economy by examining events in auto industry history, their impact on the economy, and how the economy has directly impacted the business. Then, we'll look at economic history decade-by-decade. Finally, we'll present tools and approaches to build the reader's knowledge and ability to "track" economics.

When the Ford Highland Park Plant was built in 1913 and the first mass-produced automobiles were assembled, the U.S. economy was still largely agrarian-based. There was, as yet, no real middle class in our society capable of purchasing these products in large volume. Industrialization was in its infancy. Henry Ford's basic idea was to offer highly affordable, easy-to-maintain transportation at a price any farmer or working man could afford. In fact, the Model-T was **reduced** in price regularly during the nearly two decades of its illustrious life.

The early Fords, like the early GMs and other models, were paid for in one way—COD. There were no financing contracts, insurance, or complex policies to worry about. And with prices dropping annually, interest rates and inflation were not yet concerns.

In 1914, prior to World War I, the U.S. was not really part of a global trade economy. There was certainly no trade deficit, and much of the world and its economy existed in relative isolation. In 1913 the idea of an income tax to support the Federal Government was a brand new concept and the concepts of deductible interest, business expenses, and tax avoidance strategies were unknown ideas for a distant future. But, in a dramatically changing world, everyone found themselves responsible for the cost of a free society. So taxation in the form of a federal income tax, and its impact on personal saving and business investment were added to the "economic mix" in 1913.

The typical corporation of the late 1890s and early 1900s was a holding company of loosely-held, independent business units. The management wanted the flexibility to buy/sell quickly and at a profit. (William Durant started GM in just this way.) The concept of manipulating industries to create monopolies was an accepted business strategy. American business was largely driven by a small group of phenomenally wealthy financiers like Dupont, Morgan, and the Rockefellers.

Ironically, it was Henry Ford with his $5 day in 1914 that began to turn all this around. Escalating prices (a new idea called inflation) and an interactive world economy soon became realities after World War I. Centuries of political and economic isolation were coming to an end. The value of one nation's currency and desirability of its products were coming into balance with the ability of other nations to purchase those products. The developing balance became the new driver of a young worldwide economy.

In 1919, a world newly at peace following the Treaty of Versailles and the end of World War I, found itself in a world-wide economic depression, with much of its economy collapsed, just at a time when the war had moved the world to an industrialized, manufacturing-based economy. Many of the numerous, small "cottage" automakers of the period went bankrupt. In 1920, the General Motors Board of Directors and their financing banks forced out William Durant as Chairman (for the second time) and brought in Pierre Dupont to replace him. Dupont, in turn, brought in Alfred P. Sloan to reorganize the young conglomerate. This change was to be one of the most significant in American business history, the change from a number of independent entities in a massive holding company to a tightly integrated "command control," vertical corporation, with centralized procedures, policy, finance, and research. It would change American (and world) business, and the economy, forever.

In the first GM reorganization, between 1920 and 1926, Sloan brought about numerous economic innovations: the Dealer Operating Report; the idea that return-on-investment to the shareholders was the principal job of management; the importance of reasonable return-on-investment and on assets to the Dealer; financing the customer's purchase over time; the importance of significant investment in research and development; a product development core organization; and a standard accounting system, driven by an annual budget process. By 1926, with its reorganization complete, GM was ready to vie seriously with Ford for dominance in the world automotive market. From 1923 to 1929, both companies were to experience record-breaking sales in a booming economy not unlike the 1980s.

Following this period of prosperity, the effects of margin buying of stocks, trade restrictions, and sudden overcapacity in a number of young industries brought on the stock market crash of October 1929, and resulted in the depression of the 1930s. This was the period of deepest economic failure in modern history, which brought hard times to all world industries for over a decade. The idea that a plunging stock market could bring about national deflation and mass economic failures in banking, as well as manufacturing, illustrated how fully integrated the U.S. and world economy was becoming, with public ownership of business becoming the norm (as opposed to the private ownership so commonplace in the first quarter of the twentieth century).

The New Deal of the 1930s ushered in the era of the Federal Government as the largest employer in the country. With this came the growth of spending, taxation, and public assistance programs (which came to be called "entitlements"). In the same period, the European economic collapse brought about the growth of fascism, military governments and the Axis powers in Germany, Italy, and Japan. This happened as Japan steadily expanded in the Pacific and

Asia during the decade. And slowly, America began emerging as a world leader—economically and militarily.

While President Roosevelt's New Deal program helped relieve much of the economic suffering of the country in the 1930s, it was World War II that finally brought an abrupt end to the depression and replaced it with a wartime economy, gas and critical materials rationing, and nearly complete replacement of the working force with American women. By 1943, unemployment had dropped from nearly 35% to less than 15%, and business profits had increased by nearly 60%. There was virtually a 100% demand for industrial capacity. As is usually the case in a wartime economy, great emphasis was placed on research and development, resulting in intense technological studies in manufacturing process and product design. Some of the greatest advancements were made in automobiles and trucks—advancements that would be carried over into peacetime.

Between 1941 and 1946, no new model cars were made. But with the end of the war and the conversion back to a peacetime economy, the auto industry began a unique period of technological surge and high demand. Many new techniques in manufacturing, materials, and vehicle systems were introduced. Longer term financing, the importance of warranties, and the economic impact of the "baby boomers" began to be felt.

The art of management got as much attention as did technology, with the implementation of the "Whiz Kids" at Ford Motor Company (a group of management and economic experts from the Air Corps and War Production Board) under Henry Ford II, bringing military materials, production innovations, and expediting techniques to manufacturing. In addition they brought great emphasis on new concepts in advertising and marketing, to recapture a buying public lost during the war years, and now ready to reenter the automotive marketplace under strong pent-up buying demand.

The 1950s, 60s and early 70s established the three to five year business economic cycles, with good and bad times alternating at about a three-to-one ratio in favor of prosperity over recession. The good, or "up" cycles featured high sales volume, stock value growth, profits and dividends for all. Employment was high and income increases were plentiful, which spurred buying, savings, and business and personal investments. In the auto industry, sales volumes were high, and the demand for new models and features was high. And the advertising that supported this growth fueled the development of the electronic media that carried the message, particularly the exciting new medium of television. Ironically, this development would bring about much negative publicity to the industry as well.

The "down" economic/business cycles caused consumers to hold onto their cars and trucks, and found Dealers depending on service and parts business to keep the doors open, waiting for the "good times" to return.

Sharp economic swings brought about a relatively new effect, inflation, that rose when business "heated up," increasing demand and prices, and which dramatically affected interest and made financing difficult both for buyers and manufacturers.

Another feature of the period that would have dramatic economic effects was the "pattern" labor union contracts, in which the "Big Three" manufacturer that was targeted by the union and settled first, set the "pattern" for the rest of the industry. This pattern brought about dramatic pay and benefit increases every three years, often without accompanying increases in productivity and quality. The costly results of this situation would become obvious by the late 1970s, when domestic costs of production were far greater than their foreign competition. During this period, labor contracts combined with the impacts of high demand to drive a steady increase in manufacturers' costs and prices. This produced prosperity and relatively few problems through the 60s. But when the Japanese mounted their serious entry into the market in the 70s, combined with the Arab oil crises, and the effects of spiraling inflation, interest, and debt, the domestic cost disadvantage in labor, materials, and process costs began to take a tremendous toll on the American industry and economy. (And in no industry was the impact greater than automotive.)

In the early 1980s, following a period of deep recession from 1978 to 1981, which saw the first annual losses in the corporation in 60 years, GM began a massive reorganization that would significantly change its structure for the first time since Sloan's reorganization of 1926. The GM reorganization featured, in addition to realignment into manufacturing groups, a huge investment in automation and robotics. As it turned out, this investment would probably have been better devoted to product development, Dealer network rebuilding, personnel education and customer services.

The Japanese, during this period, gained further advantage through the value of the yen vs. the dollar and as a result of the American trade deficit. They made huge investments in American bonds and property, while underselling American prices. And the first charges of "dumping," or selling in U.S. markets at below cost, were made against the Japanese auto industry. They also made impressive quality gains, "Americanized" their products, began focusing on the customer, and made their entries into the luxury and truck markets.

A parallel development was additional European and Eastern foreign investment in American debt markets, including American municipal and government bonds. This further cemented the interactive global economy with more common ownership of the world's assets, and the resulting subjection of American industry to worldwide economic, social, and political conditions.

In the late 1980s, with the impact of the truly global economy and intensive competition in every industry and every world market, a number of key events took place. The European Economic Community and North American Free Trade Agreement (in 1993) led the way to a new set of economic rules and concerns, in particular, new levels of protectionism, importing of cheaper labor, and exporting of jobs "offshore" to less expensive markets. Most of the world's traditional economic leading nations, with the United States, Canada and Great Britain in the forefront, found themselves in trade and economic deficit positions. (In Canada, for example, their deficit is as large as the country's GDP!) Financing this debt has put a great strain on the economies of the countries affected, and caused major political shifts, as national priorities shifted away from defense into private market products and services.

Many of the world's largest manufacturing corporations, in intense competition with Japanese organizations, found themselves in the position of having to dramatically improve **both** quality and productivity, and of having to shift their competitive focus to identifying and responding to customer requirements and increased owner loyalty. It was becoming increasingly obvious that the vertical "command-control" corporation, so successful in the 1920s through the 1960s, was no longer correct for the priorities of the 1970s and 1980s. This meant that many of the U.S. Fortune 50 companies, including GM, had to greatly reduce size and cut all costs, while increasing their ability to develop and introduce new products that were better, cheaper, easier to maintain, more reliable, and of superior styling. An interesting result of this is that traditional manufacturing industries, like automotive, have evolved from a pure manufacturing to a "manufacturing-service process" strategy base, with the array of customer services surrounding the product becoming as important as the product itself!

The hardest hit segment of the business population in this paradigm shift in world manufacturing has been middle management, and the economic middle class that populates the middle management ranks. The well educated, well compensated middle class is virtually disappearing from the economy as every major corporation is forced to dramatically increase efficiency and cut costs. This has resulted in a "flattening" of organizations through increased span of control and fewer managers and supervisors, leaving companies with front-line workers and executive strategists and little in between. The early 1990s see virtually all companies, manufacturing and service alike, in the process of "reengineering," examining their business processes, information management, and structure to find ways to improve productivity, cut costs, cut cycle-times, and improve response to market.

With the European Economic Community and North American Free Trade Markets, and the potential for an Asian Trade Consortium, low-cost/low-skill labor is displacing entry-level positions throughout the economy of many nations, including the U.S. A result has been an intense need for reeducation and training of displaced workers at entry levels, but also of skilled tradesmen and managers. A new class of high-tech automated machine tool operators and robotics maintenance specialists is being born in this process.

Another effect of the competitively driven economic shift has been the emergence of the service-based economy. This phenomenon has effectively converted old-line manufacturing companies (like GM) into customer-service-driven organizations, competing on a customer satisfaction/owner loyalty playing field. And it has expanded the concept of the company's "product" to include the customer services support process, throughout the complete ownership cycle, from first awareness of the product, through ownership and to the decision to repurchase.

With the expense of mass-media advertising and the increase in competitive choice available, customer **retention** has become the most important strategic marketing goal in the new world marketplace. The entry of more quality players into markets along with the prohibitive expense of mass-media advertising has helped to drive this.

One of the most important results of the high competition/free market economic developments, with their dramatic cuts into the middle class, has been the limiting of the available customer base for big ticket items like housing and new automobiles. At the same time, these markets have been segmenting—breaking down into smaller groupings with precisely defined needs—as customers seek out competitive choices that most precisely meet their needs and expectations.

One phenomenon that has emerged in this situation has been the importance of word-of-mouth advertising. To see just how important this is, let's look at some numbers that describe the "unhappy customer." Of customers with problems, fully 60% won't bother to complain to a company they're unhappy with, either because they feel it isn't worth the effort, the business is unresponsive, or they just don't know how (to complain). Of the 60% who don't complain, only 10% repurchase. Of the 40% who **do** complain and at least talk to the manufacturer, but **aren't** satisfied, 40% **still** repurchase. And, of the people who complain and **are** satisfied, fully 80% repurchase! Unhappy people who don't complain, however, aren't silent. They tell an average of 16 people about their negative experiences. And the importance of word-of-mouth is the strongest source of influence on buyers in the industry, influencing fully 32% of **all** buying decisions. This means word-of-mouth advertising has the potential of being significantly more powerful than traditional mass media advertising!

The shrinking size of available markets, lower-cost high quality competitors, knowledgeable customers with broader choice, high pressure consumer groups, "combative" media (especially the tabloid press), economic markets highly subject to the continual changes in corporations, interdependent global economic alignments, active shareholders driving boards to "manage" companies—all of these things are elements of massively changing world economic conditions.

In economic downturns, pressure for **both** customer satisfaction and warranty cost-management control in the auto industry increases. Customers become more demanding in hard times; they must keep older vehicles running, and they're especially sensitive to the price of replacement vehicles and expensive major repairs. This simply recognizes a desperate need for both immediate cash flow and long-term repeat buyers. The importance of customer retention is arguably the single, most important issue facing auto companies and, in fact, all industries today, since the average firm loses 10-30% of its customer base per year. And the cost of replacing these lost customers is six times as much as retaining them! People who don't buy new vehicles during economic slumps must keep their current cars and trucks operational so **both** warranty and customer-pay demand increases, offering the well prepared, well trained Dealer significant income opportunities that can help offset lower vehicle sales. This is also the opportunity to please and retain more customers. This situation underlines the vital importance of strong service and parts operations for successful, profitable dealerships.

Dealers also become more demanding in hard times. Lower vehicle sales volume puts intense pressure on their fixed (Service and Parts) operations; they look to the factory for assistance in all areas—warranty reimbursement, technical consultation, management help, pricing breaks in vehicles and parts, and locating top technicians. And one of the greatest challenges facing the Dealer (and industry) is how to drive down the "cost-to-retail" per unit, to free up capital that could be better invested in the customer (and turned into profits).

In hard times, it's also tougher for Dealers to turn to bank lines-of-credit for operating capital. Banks will demand pay-downs, higher interest, and stricter documentation for using credit, including personal guarantees from the Dealer Principals. In fact, cash flow becomes a top priority for all three parties—Dealer, customer and factory. Higher interest rates make financing more difficult, both for Dealers and for customers. The impact of high inflation/high interest also lowers the amount businesses can reinvest in growth. And lower profits hurt the manufacturer's ability to help ease the Dealers' financial burden.

In all cases, pressure on warranty increases greatly; prompt reimbursement, better quality fixes, parts availability, and owner demand are all factors, and unfortunately, the tendency is to "load" more into warranty increases. So, the poor economic situation exerts constant pressure on automakers to improve productivity and to cut unit costs while increasing quality. And interestingly, even with a return to prosperity, the higher level of demands doesn't fall back. Demands are simply "reset" to higher levels, reflecting a constant increase in customer expectations and requirements. All these things point to the need for a "re-appreciation" of the customer, and a strong external customer-focus strategy.

The intensely competitive economy causes constant focus on value of the yen vs. the dollar, which can put U.S. manufacturers at a price disadvantage (or improve the situation, as it has when the Japanese economy hit a downturn). The economies are dealing with a new interdependence.

In economic downturns, Dealers as well as manufacturers are apt to cut "non-productive" employes. Unfortunately, these are often the people who work with customers, train dealership employes, and process warranties—functions Dealers can least afford to lose. This increases the demand for the manufacturer's Wholesale support of the Dealer at a time when manufacturers' Field staffs are also being cut back.

Since training expense is another area often cut back in hard economic times, the Dealer's ability to provide technical service, customer support, and resources management suffers. Overall, at a time when the opportunity to increase customer loyalty is greatest, Dealers and manufacturers tend to tighten the purse strings, interpret warranty more strictly, and eliminate what really can be essential customer support functions. Dealerships become less productive and less able to support the customer.

In the automotive business, economic downturns demand discipline in managing warranty, controlling expenses, and sharpening fixed operations on the part of the Dealer. A very profitable service and parts operation allows Dealers to offer better new and used vehicle pricing, not to mention keeping the doors open by covering fixed costs and generating profits as unit sales drop. As economic conditions and competition intensify, manufacturers have become increasingly involved in the finance business, including auto loans and even credit cards, as ways of increasing product sales and profit opportunities. Credit buying has increased at an exponential rate with a corresponding increase in long-term contracts, note failures and interest rate fluctuations. The value of a manufacturer's debt, when downgraded, can put the company's Dealers in a difficult position due to the higher interest rate they must charge on financing, and often makes it impossible to finance used vehicles at all. This puts Dealers at a disadvantage in rental and leasing as well, also costing valuable contract maintenance opportunities. The global economy is forcing more offshore parts and vehicle production in a constant search for cost-cutting.

For manufacturers, this combination of situations can cause an inability to raise capital through bonds, and it also puts great pressure on the manufacturer's stock to develop both yield and capital gains.

All in all, we find ourselves in economic times far, far more difficult and complex than those facing Alfred Sloan in 1923. The same competition that has driven product quality and customer satisfaction to even higher demand levels is driving world economic competition and the changing dynamics of the auto industry. Next we'll look at the importance of understanding economic principles and a decade-by-decade analysis of the economy and its impact on the auto industry.

Why Consider Economics?

A major section of this book is devoted to understanding the economy of the U.S. (and to a lesser extent, the world) in this century. A logical question would be: Why do we devote so much text, and place so much emphasis on economics in a book on the U.S. automotive industry and on General Motors' role in the industry? The answer is that there are many reasons why economics and the workings of the economy are at the very core of understanding the industry. Here are the most important:

- No other area has had a greater impact on the automobile industry in the past 100 years than the economy and economic theory. Since the auto industry has, more than any other, been responsible for a worldwide shift from an agrarian to an industrial society, economic theory and history and the industry's business theory and history are completely intertwined, and have in many respects driven one another. So a sense of **both** histories, and understanding of major events in **each** area, automotive and economics, and how those events **impacted** one another is fundamental to understanding this business.

- The auto industry developed as it has, and Sloan's master design worked as it did because the business was born and evolved in a free-enterprise system. Its operation and its development are firmly based on a free-market system and capitalistic economy. So, how this system works tells us a great deal about the logic behind the auto industry's growth and its probable directions for the future.

- Since the automotive business is so capital-intensive, requiring very large investments by both manufacturer and retailer, economic conditions are a major determinant of the business' health. In like manner, since the automobile is second only to the home as a personal investment, and since the industry is responsible for moving more than 80% of the world's commerce, understanding the economic system is basic to understanding how and why the industry functions.

- The evolution of the automobile has had a major impact on more than the industrialization of our economy. It is a part of our social, historical, political and business development as a nation. Understanding how the industry is related to all these areas and how they interact to impact the industry is largely an economic concern. Economics is, without question, the most important business environment factor impacting the automotive industry.

- Economic theory and cycles **strongly** impact how GM and other automobile manufacturers make decisions, set priorities and direct strategy. Again, because of the business' capital intensive nature and because of the size of the automotive purchase and the economy's impact on that purchase, the theory of basic economics and business cycles must be understood.

- An understanding of economics, economic history and economic directions is most important in understanding competitors' actions, and in **predicting** their probable actions—a key to any successful business strategy.

- Understanding economic history is the best tool we have for understanding **where** the economic situation is likely to go, and **how** its direction will likely impact business.

In short, nothing is more important to the automotive business today than the economy and the effects that it has on **every** area of the business—on General Motors, the Dealers, the customers, the supplier network, and the industries supported by the transportation industry that, in turn, support it. And, the economy has a dramatic impact on **each one of us**, as employes and as consumers.

Before the 1970s, it was possible to isolate many of these issues—social, political, environmental, business, and economic. But today, manufacturers (and **all** consumers) must know more and adapt faster. And they must have an **external** focus, beyond the business, on all of the things that impact the marketplace and customer. This is true of virtually **all** business in the 1990s, not just automotive. A working knowledge of the things that impact the marketplace and customer, i.e., a working knowledge of the economy and economics, is one of the best ways to develop this focus.

The 1920s

In the decade following World War I, the United States found itself in a new role as a world leader. While the country had clearly established itself as a military power, it was strongly isolationist in many of its trade practices. At the same time the nation was developing its position as an export leader, it initiated a series of strong tariffs (particularly the Hawley Smoot Tariff) to limit imports and protect the national economy. The national mood was one of protectionism and "America first."

The decade of the 1920s was generally one of great prosperity (agriculture became one major exception by the mid-20s) as the transition from an agrarian to an industrial society progressed. And in the developing industrial society, Ford Motor Company and General Motors were the dominant world companies. In just over a decade, they had become the largest, most profitable businesses the world had ever seen. And they were rapidly becoming the main drivers of much of the country's industry and the principal sources of its economic growth.

As commerce developed, the nation's infrastructure was under construction everywhere. In direct parallel, urban development and the growth of the middle class were changing population migration and spreading wealth over a much broader social base. For the first time, the workers in the country's factories were able to buy the products they built, fueling rapid economic growth and expansion.

The many new and growing corporations were consolidating operations, developing new technologies to support the evolving transportation industry (cars, trucks, ships, and aircraft), and "reengineering" organizational structures and business processes. In many ways, the business development of the decade was similar to the 1990s. But the reasons were different. The nineteenth-century-style holding company structures were being replaced by command-control, i.e., vertically integrated corporations more suited to mass-production-based manufacturing industries. In this industrial restructuring, Alfred Sloan's design made GM the leader among modern, vertically-integrated organizations. Surrounding the huge, multi-site manufacturing complexes was a rapidly growing network of suppliers for parts and components. Economist Adam Smith's eighteenth century model of the free-market economy was alive, well, and growing more robustly than at any other period in recorded history.

As the previous decade had been purely manufacturing and price-driven, the 1920s were "income-driven" (a phenomenon first recognized by Sloan). Installment buying, annual new-car announcements and a developing used-vehicle market were changing the buyer's focus. Buyers were viewing large purchases like automobiles as percentages of their income that could be financed over time, like a home. This gave birth to focus on marketing and advertising as well as production and finance.

As companies like Ford and GM grew to dominate their industries, the Federal Government began some of its early business intervention practices. The income tax of 1913 and Sherman Anti-Trust Act of 1914 brought the government into the business of determining when a company was too large, controlling pricing and commerce in its business area, and deciding if it should be "broken up" to reestablish parity in competition with smaller companies. This concern would plague the auto industry's "Big Three" for decades.

As industry grew in every way and general employment, wages and prosperity grew along with it, everyone wanted to participate in the wealth. And as more and more companies became publicly owned, stock ownership was the most logical and accessible route to share in the prosperity. The stock market and the banking system saw the great opportunity this presented and responded with a system called margin buying. In this approach, the buyer put up a portion of the purchase price of each share of stock bought, and the bank financed the balance. The buyer could then use dividends and capital gains from the stock to pay off the bank's "margin" at cost plus an interest fee. As long as stocks were growing in value and making additional public offerings, the system worked well for everyone. The danger was in a broad sell-off of stock shares in which banks would call in their margin notes to protect their investments. This, of course, led to accelerated selling of shares and defaults, contributing strongly to the stock market crash that ended the decade.

As business, spending and investment grew during the decade, demand increased rapidly for new goods and services, and of course for the money necessary to finance this growth. In this type of economic growth cycle, inflation and interest rates keep pace. By the late 1920s, interest rates had exceeded 20%. Between accelerated margin buying of stocks, rapidly growing debt (with disproportionately low savings), a growing backlash from the rest of the world in response to high protectionist tariffs, and supply suddenly exceeding demand, the economy was poised for a major failure. We'll see exactly how this occurred in the start of the "Great Depression."

1929—The Great Crash and The Great Depression

After almost a decade of prosperity and economic growth, conditions were developing rapidly by 1929 for a downturn. Few realized at the time that it would be the worst economic crisis in our country's (and the world's) history, and would last for 12 years. A noted economist, John Kenneth Galbraith, said in his book *The Great Crash*, "Like 1066, 1776, and 1914, 1929 was a year that every one remembers." 1929 marked the point of change from the period of the greatest economic prosperity in the nation's history to the period of its greatest economic collapse.

By the late 1920s, the relatively widespread public ownership of stock, by the new middle class as well as the traditional affluent class, was still a new phenomenon. Remember, the country was still only a decade removed from the age of closely-held and privately owned holding-company structures. During the 1920s, while industry was growing rapidly and profits were keeping pace, the broad middle class—while certainly more affluent than their unskilled laborer counterparts at the turn of the century—were **not** receiving wage increases in proportion to the rapid economic growth. During the decade, nearly two-thirds of the country's families had annual incomes of less than $2,000, while the average family income for the bottom 40% of the population was only $725 per year. So, low wages tended to restrict the worker's share in the nation's prosperity, since they were limited in their ability to consume the products of American industry and agriculture. The resulting situation was this: we had a strong economy with a high level of affluence and income at the top of the economic pyramid, and high employment at the base of the pyramid, but without the capital to participate in the prosperity proportional to their contribution.

So leading right up to mid-1929, the nation was very prosperous, business was growing rapidly and profits were very high. Reinvestment in business development and the infrastructure was also high. Taxes were very low, as was inflation. As a matter of fact, since average worker wages were increasing far slower than the general economy, there was "deflation" in the economy. Productivity, overall, was up 43% in 1929 over 1919 levels. However wages were lagging behind profits, so, instead of rising, costs fell. This drove additional profits back into the hands of business, driving more investment and easy credit. This business growth scenario combined with disproportionately low salary growth set the stage for falling consumer consumption by mid-1929, while interest rates fueling margin buying rose rapidly, pressuring both business and private investment.

Due to high profit, controlled essentially by the new industrialists and bankers, credit was readily available and the general "mood" of the times was very upbeat. The American public idolized and trusted the "captains of industry" like Henry Ford, Alfred Sloan, and Walter Chrysler. It was not like the politically and economically cynical world of the 1990s. America was ready and willing to put itself in the hands of its new generation of business leaders, and was seeking a way to share in the prosperity—a way not readily available through their working income. Wall Street and the stock market was a new and exciting path to share in this prosperity.

Driven by the confidence and optimism of the times, totally trusting of the industrialists and bankers, the new middle class needed only a means to share in the wealth. This was provided in the form of margin buying. With the huge demands for borrowing, interest rates rose very rapidly right along with the booming demand. Then, while the borrowers took their time repaying margin loans, they were able to receive the full benefits of 100% stock ownership—capital gains, interest, and dividends. In the high profit growth climate of the mid-1920s, the total return on the stock investment more than paid the margin interest rates and still left a profit for the new investors.

Given this scenario, by 1928 margin buying had reached a level of 50:1 (an investor could borrow $50 for a $1 investment to purchase stock), and interest rates had climbed over 20%. There was, in effect, an even greater transfer of wealth to the industrialists and bankers. But, there was a rapidly falling level of real, tangible assets to support stock prices. The market was becoming highly overpriced and real liquidity (ability to readily convert assets to cash) was falling. In addition, the protectionist/isolationist attitude with its high tariffs was making it even harder for Europe and Asia to export their goods to the U.S., and without the resulting income, it was harder for them to purchase U.S. goods or service their World War I debts owed to the U.S. The ultimate results of this situation were that by mid-1929, consumer demand for goods was falling and inventories continued growing far longer than supply-demand logic would normally dictate.

The Federal Reserve Index of industrial activity, the best measure of economic activity available in the 1920s, peaked at an all-time high in June 1929. At this point, a steady decline set in, and the economy was weakening rapidly by the Fall of 1929. At this point, production in the new factories had outpaced demand (governed, remember, by the relatively stable income levels that were falling behind industrial growth and profit levels). But, industry misread the signs and kept building on its unsold inventories. Then, on October 24, 1929, a massive sell-off of stocks began. This drove banks to begin calling in their margin notes. As a result, millions were ruined financially as their ownings were liquidated at rapidly falling rates as they tried to cover their margin notes. Of course, with stock prices tumbling, there was simply too little liquidity to zero the amount of debt in the system. Financiers like Morgan and DuPont did what they could to salvage the situation, buying stocks rapidly to pump capital into the system, but it was too little, too late. As a result, the stock market lost fully half of its value in 24 hours. The impact on the economy was immediate and awesome.

In September 1929, there were 45 million people employed in the U.S. By the end of the year, in just two months, 15 million of these jobs were lost. The Gross National Product (sum of all economic activity—revenues and income) in the United States was $80 billion. By 1932, it was cut by 50%, to $40 billion. This economic catastrophe demonstrated the power that Wall Street and the financial markets had gained over the national economy in less than two decades.

It took until 1937 for the nation's production volume to return to 1929 levels. And even then, the recovery was **very** brief. By 1938, nine years after the stock market crash, one in five Americans was still unemployed, nearly four times the level of a normal healthy economy.

The stock market crash in 1929, then, was due in large part to speculation fueled by margin buying. Stock values were **not** driven up by economic performance and normal business growth cyclic patterns of rising consumption and supply driving employment, which in turn drives up prices and inflation. Once the market fall began, there were no economic "value dynamics" to stop it—**all** stocks were clearly overvalued. The resulting depression was so deep that new investment in business, with its economic recovery, would be curtailed for the longest period in the nation's history.

There were five key indicators of trouble prior to the depression.

1. The **distribution of income:** In the 1920s, five percent of the population received 35 percent of all personal income. This made the economy more dependent on consumer spending in the non-durable goods areas. This is where the majority of income is distributed in a strong economy, but not where the very affluent, regardless of their wealth, can or will spend enough to offset low levels of middle class spending.

2. In much of industry, **inept holding companies were still managing business**, particularly in utilities, railroads, and entertainment. The interruption of dividends due to poor financial management caused the bonds of these companies to default in large numbers, causing many bankruptcies. Income had to be used for debt payment and not investment. This contributed to a **deflation** economy.

3. The **banking structure**. There were so many independent banks that, when one failed, depositors began pulling out of other, non-affiliated banks in a panic. There was no real network of financial support, as exists today, between banks. This made bank failures very common and magnified the panic effect on society.

4. **High tariffs** on foreign imports caused a high U.S. export surplus. This meant that countries that had very large debts to the U.S. from World War I couldn't make their payments. There began to be many defaults. This, in turn, caused a fall in our export trade since these countries could not afford U.S. goods.

5. The federal focus was on **balancing the budget** after the crash—at the expense of tax cuts and other measures that would have supported business investment and economic recovery.

As a result of these things, factory orders declined into the 1930s and unemployment rose rapidly and fed upon itself. The economy of 1929 was fundamentally weak, and the fear caused by the crash was so widespread, that business and consumers were afraid of spending for years afterward. In Europe, the situation caused collapse of the German economy and others. The currency inflation and debt default that took place paved the way for the growth of Adolf Hitler's National Socialist Party (Nazis). Further, in the 1930s, the U.S. diverted fuel and steel from Japan to our national markets. Ultimately, these events would pave the way for the scenario that led to World War II.

The 1930s

The Great Depression, brought on by the Stock Market Crash of 1929, would continue throughout the decade of the 1930s—the most prolonged economic disaster in world history. America and the world were desperately poor. In most periods of recession, finding a job becomes the top priority, and in most recessions unemployment seldom exceeds 10%. In the Great Depression, unemployment reached as high as 33% and survival was the priority. The Federal Government's approach under President Herbert Hoover was to focus all efforts on balancing the federal budget. Measures normally taken in economic slumps to stimulate business, like tax cuts, investment credits, government spending on national projects to add to the workforce (prior to 1933), etc., were not taken.

By the early 1930s, the value of American businesses, in the form of stocks, had dropped to less than half of the value they had reached in the late 1920s. Industrial production declined rapidly; consumerism virtually ceased. Many banks and businesses failed; income—particularly in the new middle class—declined rapidly, and industrial production had dropped to less than half of the 1929 levels by 1932.

The Federal Government's responses under President Herbert Hoover between 1930 and 1932 were very small scale, and were focused on industry and banks. However, business stimulation remained low as Hoover kept the economic priorities on balancing the budget, and refused to inflate currency or abandon the gold standard (i.e., that there must be one dollar in gold for each paper dollar released into the system). And during this early part of the depression, the government refused to provide any direct relief to the unemployed.

By 1932, factory wages in the United States had dropped by 60 percent. At the same time the national debt had increased from $16.2 billion to $22.5 billion. Agriculture was the hardest hit of any sector of the economy, having been in a deep depression since the early 1920s, well before the rest of the economy. Banks and other financial institutions were also among the first areas to be impacted by the collapse of the economy, being initially hit by the huge amount of margin loan failures. In early 1933, banks in 22 states closed to avoid collapse, an event that started in Michigan and came to known as the "Bank Holiday." President Hoover's last action to combat the depression was establishing the Reconstruction Finance Corporation (RFC) in 1932, to provide bank and business loans and to combat deflation.

In 1932, Franklin D. Roosevelt ran for the Presidency against Hoover on a platform of direct government relief for the unemployed. This was a powerful position since it offered an incentive directly to those hardest hit by the depression. It also addressed one of the most important aspects of the Great Depression, the terrible emotional burden and sense of frustration and helplessness that were prevalent throughout all levels of society. This was in direct contrast to the administration's approach of balancing the budget, providing limited assistance directly to business and banking, and verbally urging people and business not to fear the economic situation, but to spend and invest. Roosevelt won the election by a wide margin.

President Roosevelt's program to end the depression was called the "New Deal." It was based on intense, direct stimulation of the economy through direct aid to those hardest hit. Here's the background and philosophy behind the "New Deal."

- Its foundation lay in the work of the British economist, John M. Keynes. Keynes' approach advocated strong government regulation of banking and private business. It also called for federal control of the monetary system and the supply of money in the economy. The approach took the country off the gold standard and put the Federal Reserve Board directly in control of the money supply, with the ability to inflate or deflate the economy through direct control of the amount of currency available.

- The New Deal created the Central Banking System (which has since come to be called the Federal Reserve Board) with the authority to inflate or deflate currency in order to control interest rates and, as a result, to help drive investment by making more money available to business and individuals at lower interest rates. The **basic philosophy** was to control economic activity—inflation, money supply, interest rates, deficit and debt—outside the normal effect of free-market forces through taxation and a system of economic "entitlements." These entitlements involved a transfer of wealth from one section of the economy to others under direct government supervision. Entitlements included public jobs creation, social security, public education, the welfare system, early health care initiatives, and a host of other programs. These entitlements became government "industries" that could control competition outside the normal economic controls of the free-market. This allowed price, efficiency, and production levels control, but prevented business growth that normally results from open private-sector competition.

In the first 100 days of the Roosevelt presidency, the New Deal saw more economic support programs created than in any other period before or since. The most important of these programs were:

- The Civilian Conservation Corps (CCC)—designed to employ 18 to 25-year-olds in the forest service, national parks renovation, and other conservation-oriented areas.

- The Federal Emergency Relief Act—provided matching federal funds for state and locally originated programs.

- The Agricultural Adjustment Act—to provide subsidies to farmers for regulating what crops they raised and how much of each crop farmers could produce.

- The Tennessee Valley Authority (TVA)—a program to develop dams and water control for generating electric power across seven southern states.

- The Home Owners' Loan Act—to provide refinancing of private home mortgages at lower interest rates.

- The Farm Credit Act—to provide similar lower interest refinancing for farm mortgage loans.

- The Glass-Steagall Banking Act—separated commercial and investment banking to limit the kind of speculation abuse that helped cause the stock market crash in 1929.

- The National Industrial Recovery Act (NIRA)—to regulate industry practices and production rates.

- The Public Works Administration—to create jobs through building the nation's infrastructure based on a massive program of road and highway building.

The "Second New Deal" was then launched in 1935 to greatly expand the new system of federal relief programs by adding a number of new economic supports and entitlements. The most important of these was the Social Security Act, which established a mandatory national pension retirement plan, and which would become the longest surviving New Deal program.

Roosevelt's New Deal did three things:

1. It provided desperately needed temporary relief for the unemployed and impoverished.

2. It helped re-establish confidence in a nation battered by economic hardship and afraid to hire, expand, spend or invest.

3. It paved the way for a greatly expanded role of the Federal Government in managing the economy.

In the short-term, Roosevelt's New Deal was quite successful. In fact, it drove a "mini recovery" of the economy by 1937 (which, however, proved to be very short-lived). Perhaps the most important accomplishment of the New Deal was to restore the public's faith in the economy. One of the main outcomes of the depression was the fear, and the unwillingness to invest or spend the capital that was available. This was as damaging as the actual economic dynamics.

In the long-term, the "temporary" federal programs were meant to "fix" the economy, and then place it back in the hands of publically-owned free enterprise; but some programs became much longer term, and in some cases, permanent. This assumes that government is more skilled at business management and capital production than private enterprise. It also created the long-term effect of expanding government regulation and intervention in private industry. Finally, it set the stage for a great expansion in the size of government. All of this created questions and concerns we are trying to deal with today, some 60 years later.

A final product of the economically tumultuous 1930s, and one that would continue to have a major impact on our society even now was the growing labor unrest and the responding growth of labor unions. This growth began in 1935 when a spin-off group from the American Federation of Labor (AFL) that represented craftsmen, formed the Committee for Industrial Organization (CIO) to represent industrial factory workers. In December 1936, the United Auto Workers (UAW), an affiliate of the CIO, launched a strike against GM. This strike lasted until mid-February in 1937, and resulted in General Motors being the first automaker to recognize the union. Membership grew rapidly, from seven million unionized workers in 1937 to 10.5 million members by the start of World War II in 1941, the year in which Ford Motor Company became the final automaker to admit the union.

The 1940s

Franklin Roosevelt's "New Deal" legislation helped to ease the impact of the Great Depression, and restore the country's confidence in the economy. But it was World War II in 1941 that finally ended the Great Depression. Ironically World War II was largely a product of the economic and political changes caused by the depression, changes even more dramatic in Germany and Japan and across all of Europe and Asia than they were in America.

As "big" wars often do, World War II caused an almost immediate "100% demand" condition for the full manufacturing capacity of the country. At the same time, between military service and the massive requirements for war materials, it caused a huge drop in unemployment. By early 1942, unemployment, which had been at 33% in 1933, was cut to 15% in just a few months. It would fall below 5% by 1944, with women and draft-deferred men being called on to fill the seven-day, three-shift factory demands for military armaments.

The War also served to strongly regulate industry, through the use of price controls and the rationing of strategic materials to ensure the availability of things like steel, rubber, and gasoline for the war effort. This regulation process caused automotive, as well as many other manufacturing industries that had been producing products for private consumption to be converted to military and munitions production.

The War was also responsible for major changes in management philosophy. This was brought about primarily by the centralized operations control unit called the War Regulations Board. This group was populated by a combination of established corporate managers and a young generation of scientific managers steeped in the mathematics of production and new productivity and quality control processes. (See Section I, Chapter 4.)

By 1943 business profits were up 57% over pre-war levels. Due to wage increases and overtime pay, wages of American workers were 50% higher in 1945 than they had been in 1939. The War also caused a great and immediate increase in demand for agricultural products, ending the depression in this, the hardest and longest suffering segment of the economy.

Roosevelt established a number of new agencies to manage wartime production and the economy:

- The War Production Board, headed by Donald M. Nelson of Sears and Roebuck, was responsible for resources mobilization.

- The Office of War Mobilization was established to supervise the war economy, under the leadership of Supreme Court Justice James F. Byrnes.

- The War Resources Board, which developed planning to convert factories from peacetime to war production, was headed by William S. Knudson from GM.

- The Office of Price Administration was established to set price ceilings and control rents and ration materials and goods. Its main purpose was to control inflation in a time of rapidly rising wages and industrial production.

Fighting World War II cost the U.S. $300 billion. A large part of the burden for funding had to come from income taxes. Personal income taxes and corporate income taxes were increased, but the Revenue Act of 1942 spread these increases over a much broader tax base (four times as many tax payers as 1939), lessening the impact on individuals.

An interesting footnote is that General Motors received fully eight percent of all government contracts during the War!

Following the War, with the occupation of Japan and the Marshall Plan for rebuilding Europe, the United States became the dominant world leader—militarily and economically—financing much of the foreign debt that came about as a result of the War.

One of the most important economic results of World War II was a huge pent-up demand for products not available during the war. Automobiles (there had been no new models between 1941 and 1945) were one of the products most in demand. There were many other good economic signs. In 1946, employment rose to 55 million, seven million more than 1940. The U.S. Gross National Product was back to the pre-depression level for the first time when it reached $100.6 billion. The "Baby Boom" was another strong stimulus for the post-war economy, with the birth rate increasing to 24 per 1000 in 1946, and remaining at that record-high rate until the 1960s. Low inflation, high employment, the broader tax bases, and the G.I. Bill all combined with pent-up demand to stimulate the economic boom that accelerated in the late 1940s. Industry investments also accelerated rapidly, going to $22 billion in 1948, an increase of 250 percent over 1945.

Three important pieces of economic legislation passed in this period that would have long-term deep impacts on the economy:

- The Employment Act of 1946 gave the Federal Government a major role in maintaining high levels of employment and economic prosperity, opening the doors for huge taxing and spending increases.

- The Taft-Hartley Act of 1947 prohibited the closed shop (only union workers), but permitted the union shop (a worker when hired **would** be required to join an already in-place union) unless banned by state law.

- Tax cuts in 1947 lowered taxes by $5 billion and removed over seven million low-income workers from income tax responsibility.

These events set a framework for both prosperity and broader government influence in the economy. In addition, the end of the 1940s saw the U.S. moving away from the isolationism of the 1930s to a role as "global policeman" from the 1950s on.

The 1950s

The prosperity of the late 1940s continued into the post-war "baby boom" decade of the 1950s. The economic dynamics of the late 1940s—pent-up growing consumer demand, high employment levels and low inflation kept growing well into the next decade. In 1952, new President Dwight D. Eisenhower, the first Republican to hold office since the defeat of Herbert Hoover by Franklin D. Roosevelt in 1932, surprised traditional party members when he demanded spending cuts before income tax reductions. He succeeded in reducing the deficit to only $3 billion, paltry by today's standards. He followed this with tax cuts of over $7 billion in 1954. Due to the Federal Reserve Board's attempts to cool inflation in the rapidly growing economy, there was a brief recession in the winter of 1953-54, but a strong, almost immediate recovery would continue for over three years.

The strong conservative government supported business investment, causing industrial investments that led to strong growth and very high corporate profits. There was a trade surplus and no real national debt problem. The United States became, in the words of economist and author John Kenneth Galbraith, an "affluent society" in the 1950s. The country's Gross National Product increased from $200 billion to $500 billion between 1954 and 1960. By mid-decade the U.S. was producing virtually half the world's goods and services. Personal income doubled in the decade, and the purchasing power of the American consumer rose by 22% between 1946 and 1960.

Automobile ownership doubled during the 1950s, and about 50,000 miles of highways were built annually from 1956 to 1960, at an annual cost of over $25 billion. The automobile strongly contributed to business growth in other industries as well. For example, the auto encouraged national franchise chain development of companies like Holiday Inns, Kentucky Fried Chicken, McDonalds, and Burger King, a phenomenon that would rapidly grow to become a major segment of the nation's economy. By 1960, there were some 50 million cars on U.S. roads!

Corporate consolidations were another feature of the 1950s economy. By 1960, less than 100 corporations controlled half the nation's corporate wealth. AT&T was the world's largest with assets of $24 billion. (It would be restructured due to anti-trust legislation in the 1980s.) General Motors was the largest manufacturer, with assets of over $13 billion. It was in the 1950s that GM's Charles Wilson made his famous (and often misquoted) statement to Congress: "What was good for our country was good for GM and vice versa."

This period also saw reductions in trade barriers, promoting expanded foreign trade. (However, as American foreign aid to post-war Europe and Asia continued to grow, it was not enough to cover our overseas expenditures and investments.)

The period of the 1950s saw the evolution of the three-to-five year economic cycles that would continue into the 1970s. These cycles worked as shown in the chart below.

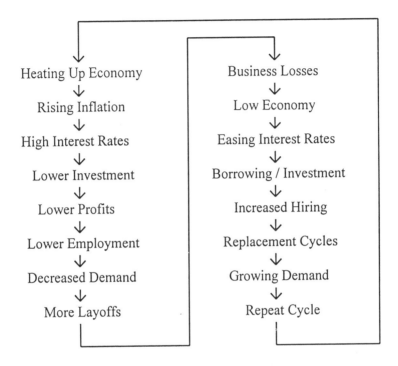

At the top of the chart we are in a strong economy that's "heating up." This leads to rising inflation that in turn leads to rising interest rates. As rates get higher, companies begin "pulling back," cutting inventories and lowering investment. At this point retained profits normally begin falling which soon leads to layoffs. With more people unemployed, demand decreases. This quickly leads to further business losses and more layoffs. By this point, most economic indicators begin to fall. Once this cycle "bottoms," interest rates begin to ease. Before long, this leads to increased borrowing and investment by business. Hiring then begins to increase. By this time, replacement cycles on durable goods are normally beginning to run their course. This, combined with rising employment, increases demand, and the cycle repeats.

The 1960s

By the late 1950s, the inflation rate, while still relatively low, had slowly started to increase. By 1961, unemployment had crept up to seven percent. New President John F. Kennedy was very concerned about inflation. So he at first hesitated to propose tax cuts to address the situation and boost the economy, since he feared that lower tax revenues would lead to growing budget deficits. When the economy remained sluggish however, on advice from the Council of Economic Advisors, Kennedy called for a $13.5 billion reduction in taxes on corporations, over three years, to boost business investment.

There was still general prosperity early in the decade. The automotive business was very successful. The manufacturing-driven principle was still very strong, with GM controlling over 60% of the market in 1963. Then, by mid-decade, major changes began to take place in world politics and economics. The two major impactors were the Vietnam conflict and the "Great Society" of President Lyndon B. Johnson, a broad new system of entitlements evolving with the sweeping civil rights reforms of the decade.

These things added $600 billion to the national debt by 1970. Much of the war expenses and the new entitlements were funded **in spite** of President Kennedy's tax cuts, adding the huge amount to the nation's debt. By late decade, taxes and interest had begun accelerating rapidly to fund a rapidly growing Federal Government, beginning a spiral of national debt.

The 1970s

With the 1970s, there finally came an abrupt end to the economic prosperity that started after World War II. While President Richard Nixon focused strongly on foreign affairs, domestically he sought to reduce the influence of the Federal Government over state and local economic affairs. He called his program the "New Federalism." Under his plan, Congress initiated a five-year plan in 1972 for revenue-sharing that would distribute $30 billion in tax revenues back to state and local governments.

In the early seventies, Social Security benefits increased for retirees, but so did Social Security taxes. And during this period, the Federal Government took on additional assistance programs for the blind and disabled that had previously been provided through joint state and federal funding. These were also funded through the growing Social Security program.

Inflation was the most pressing economic issue in 1970. To attack it, President Nixon cut government spending, while the Federal Reserve Board tightened credit and increased interest rates to slow the expansion of the money supply. In late 1970, the stock market saw its greatest fall in over 30 years, and Gross National Product declined for the first time since 1958. In the Economic Stabilization Act of 1970, Nixon began federal regulation of wages and prices. This process failed to control inflation, which rose to 9% by 1973.

Exports began declining, and the cost of importing raw materials rose at the same time; the result was the first trade deficit in 80 years. In this environment, taxes and interest began growing steadily. Then in 1973 the first OPEC Oil Crisis hit, beginning the "politics of oil" and demonstrating dramatically the arrival of the integrated world economy.

At this time the Japanese, in addition to entering the world economic arena in the auto industry, began an aggressive program of buying U.S. debt. Also at this time, a shift from equity financing (through stock issuance) to debt financing (through bond issuance) began. The U.S. faced "stagflation"—a unique combination of a stagnant economy **and** rising inflation, two economic conditions that normally move opposite one another.

Inflation doubled after 1973, and by 1978 had reached double digits. During the decade, the national debt also doubled and our trade deficits continued to accelerate. By 1975 unemployment had reached 8.5%.

As part of their aggressive economic expansion plan, the Japanese entered the U.S. auto industry, focusing on fuel economy, quality, and price. This led to charges of Japanese "dumping" (selling below cost to buy market-share) and resulted in a series of voluntary import restraints by the Japanese. Japan began building assembly plants and extensive supplier/financial networks in the United States.

By decade's end, the interest on the deficit was compounding faster than current revenues, and the country was in a deep spiral of national debt. Starting in 1976, President Jimmy Carter began focusing on lowering unemployment to correct the nation's failing economy. In addition, he set a top priority on balancing the federal budget. Both these approaches failed to correct the surging economic problems of the 1970s, and by 1980 the government budget deficit reached an all-time high of $60 billion. Mortgage rates in 1980 reached 15% and the prime interest rate (the rate banks charge their most solid investors) had risen to 20%!

The 1980s

One of the most important economic impactors of the 1980s occurred in the last year of the Carter presidency when Paul Voelker was named the head of the Federal Reserve Board. In the 80s, under President Ronald Reagan and Chairman Voelker, a policy that became known as "Reaganomics" was developed. (It would also be called, more correctly, supply-side economics; it was also known as "trickle-down economics.") In this approach, the focus was on cutting back on the scope and economic influence of the Federal Government, and reducing social entitlements, shifting the burden of prosperity back to the free-market system and private industry. The objective was to control inflation through money supply management and tax reductions, making lower interest loans to key industries and lessening government intervention in business.

The basic principle of supply-side economics is that excessive taxation causes most of the economic problems in a free-market, capitalistic economy. To counteract this, Congress passed the Economic Recovery Tax Act in 1981, which cut $749 billion in taxes over five years, particularly in the upper-income brackets. The objective was to encourage the top end of the economy to invest their savings in business, ultimately producing a "trickle-down" economic benefit that would be felt throughout the economy at all income levels.

During the early 1980s, the administration also increased defense spending while cutting domestic spending, particularly the social entitlements, which were cut by $100 billion between 1980 and 1982.

Reagan's plan was to reduce taxes, spur business investment through tax cuts and deregulation of industry, increase military spending while reducing entitlements, **and**, at the same time, balance the nation's budget. Business prosperity was stimulated strongly, but balancing the budget failed. The budget deficit increased from $59 billion in 1980 to $221 billion in 1986. By 1984, the national debt was at $1.2 **trillion**, and by 1989, it had risen to $3 trillion. In 1985, the Gramm-Rudman Holings Act was passed. It was meant to force balancing the budget by 1991, but failed to accomplish this goal.

In early 1982, unemployment was at 10%, its highest level since the 1940s. Paul Voelker's Federal Reserve Board relaxed credit restrictions to boost the economy by encouraging further private investment. Inflation dropped to below 5% and unemployment to below 7% by 1986 under this plan.

By 1985, for the first time since 1914, the United States had become a debtor nation, owing more in foreign debt than was owed to us. As another element of his economic plan, President Reagan began a strong initiative to reduce the value of the dollar in order to correct the trade imbalance. As a result of this program, the dollar's value relative to foreign currency declined by 37% between 1985 and 1988.

One of the most significant events came on "Black Monday," October 19th, 1987, when the stock market, driven by high speculation and a positive mood to its highest levels ever, fell 508 points in one day. However, due to the fundamentally strong economy, this did not have the long-term impacts of the crash of 1929 that led to the Great Depression. Basically the market recovered and the strong business economy continued for another three years after "Black Monday."

In terms of overall economic strengths and weaknesses, the 1980s can be summarized as follows:

- **Positive:** The economic policies of Ronald Reagan and Paul Voelker worked well in terms of stimulating business growth. Beginning with the tax cuts of 1983, there were eight years of general prosperity and growth, one of the strongest economic development periods in our nation's history. Strong growth in the industrial, private sector stimulated the bond markets to add further opportunity to an already strong investment market.

- **Negatives:**
— The trade deficit, debt and budget deficit were the major weaknesses, along with a weak dollar. High U.S. interest rates on government bonds, meant to finance our growing debt, continued to attract Japanese and other foreign investment. This strengthened the dollar and the trade deficit widened.

— The highly speculative market conditions and strong government deregulation brought about the single most damaging economic happening of the 1980s. The environment encouraged dangerously speculative loans in the banking industry, and particularly in the Savings and Loan institutions. A group of unscrupulous investors, the most notorious of which was the group led by Charles Keating of Lincoln Savings and Loan, used the "easy-credit," lax regulation environment to make a series of massive, unsupported loans that resulted in huge profits for the people involved and the loss of billions by unsuspecting investors. In 1990, after the fraudulent practices were uncovered, the Government Accounting Office estimated that compensating investors for their losses through the Federal Savings and Loan Insurance Corporation (FSLIC) and the Federal Deposit Insurance Corporation (FDIC), would cost the American tax payers $500 billion over the next 10 to 15 years.

— The birth of "junk bonds" as a means of financing leveraged buyouts of companies brought about the second great economic scandal of the 1990s. Fueled by the same environment of encouraging speculation and discouraging regulation, junk bonds were a clever use of a corporation's own assets to finance its takeover. The process consisted of brokers putting together packages of very high-risk, high-yield bonds (buying a company's **debt** rather than its assets, in return for interest payments and an agreement to pay back the principal at some future point), that were in turn used to finance takeover of the company by a management group controlling the bond sales. This practice could make company stocks very attractive by driving up their stock prices in anticipation of a large infusion of capital into the company through the bond sales. This in turn, led to an illegal practice called "insider trading," in which the investors who knew of the bond deals in advance of the general public bought stock at lower prices and then sold it off as announcements were made of takeovers. The sell prices were often two or more times the value of the purchase price, giving the "insiders" an unfair advantage that they manipulated in the first place through the junk bond sales. The damaging results of these practices were growth unsupported by real profits and asset development, and poorly structured reorganizations with weak uninvolved managers interested only in making a "quick killing" and moving on to the next deal.

— A final negative indicator, which stretched well beyond economic issues, was discovered in a study done by the Carnegie Foundation in the mid-1980s. The report on this study was called "A Nation at Risk." Its main finding was that the U.S. educational system—elementary, high schools and colleges—was producing mediocrity. Students with high school diplomas and college degrees typically were not prepared for entry-level jobs in business, industry, science and education. This study provided a powerful warning to a country strongly dependent on superior business and technology skills, i.e., dependent on a powerful, superior educational system. As we enter the 1990s, this may yet be the greatest challenge facing our social, business and economic strengths as a nation.

The 1990s

By mid-1990, the economic downturn of the late 1980s had become a full-scale recession. Many "Fortune 50" companies were reporting large losses in profits and market-share (a particular problem in the automotive industry). This led to an occurrence not seen since 1920—Boards of Directors of these large, old firms were suddenly demanding accountability from company management. The president and chairman and senior executive staffs of GM were among the first to be "fired" by their Boards. IBM, American Express and a number of others would soon follow. It was clear that the 1990s would not accept "business as usual" performance, paying out huge executive salaries and bonuses, while losses were mounting in our biggest manufacturing and service companies.

In the presidential election year of 1992, unemployment in the U.S. had grown to 7.4%, making the economy the principal political issue. There was a strong perception that then-President George Bush focused government efforts almost exclusively on foreign affairs at the expense of domestic issues like employment (in spite of the fact that in 1991, he was in a very strong position following the Persian Gulf War and seemed all but assured of re-election).

Bill Clinton, the Democratic candidate, focused campaign efforts on the weak economy. The Republicans' bid was further weakened by the running of ultra-conservative Pat Buchanan and by independent Ross Perot, both drawing traditional Republican voters away from Bush. Clinton won the election based on commitments to address serious domestic problems, principally, crime, the weak economy and unemployment, the health-care crisis, and a growing deficit. The Congress and President were both Democratic for the first time in a dozen years. And the election marked the passage of power to the "baby boomers," born after World War II. In short, the growing national debt, strong recession, the savings and loan disaster, and flat economic growth finally led to political change.

When President Clinton took office in 1993, a slow recovery was taking place that had started in late 1992. But this recovery was far weaker than that which followed the 1981-82 recession. The economy was essentially stagnant. There was low inflation, but also very slow growth due to massive deficits in trade and budget and the national debt. The economic recovery is continuing in 1994, but at a slow rate with another year of Gross Domestic Product growth projected in the 2.8 to 3.0% range (rather than the 5.0 to 6.0% range typical of a strong recovery), with low inflation, low interest rates, and less unemployment.

One of the most important impacts of the current economy is that the persisting weaknesses are driving a strong wave of change throughout industry. This change will be analyzed regarding the auto industry in the final section of this book, "Aligning for the Future." However, there are certain characteristics of change that are holding true across all industries and major corporations. Here are some of them.

- Companies are reducing size and cutting the labor force through improved business process and productivity.

- The process of "cost-cutting" is being re-evaluated by analyzing the company's products and processes in terms of delivering optimum "value-added" to the customer, a process known as "reengineering."

- Manufacturers are shortening product development and all service activity "cycle times"—the time it takes to complete a task from input to output, thereby lowering cost and improving customer response.

- Organizational structures are becoming more "horizontal," with fewer layers of management than traditional vertical business structures have; again, the goal is to lower costs, speed decision-making and improve response.

- As part of the "horizontal" organization concept, companies are implementing cross-function teams to cut across the traditional "silo" functions, integrating processes to improve quality and delivery of goods and services.

- Front-line employes, those who deal directly with customers, are being empowered to make decisions far beyond those they could make a few years ago, and more experienced, high skill level people are being put into front-line positions.

- Businesses are looking for new ways to differentiate themselves from their competition. In a number of industries, automotive in particular, product quality has become an "entry-level" issue, rather than a differentiator. This stimulates differentiation into new areas, the most important being the expanding realm of customer services, in which process is often becoming as important as the product itself.

- All companies are going through a process of culture change, in which they are trying to realign their focus from an internal administrative priority to an external-customer priority. This is sometimes called the "culture of customer empathy."

- Many organizations are trying to "re-educate" their shareholders to the importance of accepting short-term costs to develop long-term return. Another way of saying this is that corporate boards of directors have a new role—accepting the responsibility for convincing investors that equity growth and the long-term strategic growth of the company must take precedence over short-term high dividend yields if companies are to remain innovative and competitive.

At the present time, the major global competitors, the U.S., Japan, and Germany, are all facing parallel problems regarding cost management, profitability, labor, efficient management systems, best business processes, and all the issues that determine the winning "pull"-driven company (the company that is driven by the requirements of the customer).

In response to global competitiveness, the world economy is driving toward the formation and refinement of three powerful free-trade blocks: the European Economic Community (365,000,000 customers), NAFTA (the North American Free Trade Agreement with 400,000,000 customers) and a potential Asian Consortium (with over 600,000,000 customers). Each of these blocks will try to align their partner countries to trade profitably within the blocks with minimum tariffs and trade barriers. This process is forcing a tremendous "rethink" in how economics works, how businesses function, and the "rules" for a global economy.

As this book goes to press, at the end of the first quarter, 1994, the stock and bond markets are experiencing a phenomenon which may well become a regular feature of the financial markets well into the future. In the strong "bull" market that has predominated over the past three plus years, many small independent investors have entered the investment markets through the instrument of the mutual fund—a large group of stock and/or bond holdings under central professional management. The idea of the mutual fund is to diversify holdings, spread risk, and provide professional management all in one easy-to-purchase and trade investment medium. Mutual fund "families" commonly offer aggressive-growth, growth and income, balanced, income (usually bonds), and money-market accounts—allowing the investor to fully diversify, spread risk, and meet all investment needs—from long-term growth to current income, all within the single fund family.

The mutual fund concept has become so popular that, today, mutual fund holders have become the dominant investment segment, replacing "institutional" investors that dominated stock and bond holdings just a few short years ago.

Between February and early April, 1994, the financial markets have experienced a strong "correction," common after a prolonged "bullish" period that pushes equity values much higher than companies' assets and profits would justify. At the same time, rising interest rates, characteristic of a strong economy, have caused sell-offs in the bond markets, with corresponding liquidation in the stock market. Consequently, the Federal Reserve Board has acted to "cool" the potential inflationary trend by raising the discount interest rate on two occasions. All these occurrences are quite normal results of a recovering economy, and normally cause market corrections in the 10-15% range.

However, in the "new markets" of the 1990s, with the large numbers of small investors holding the funds (easily traded in most cases through a simple 800-line call), the impacts of normal corrections in a seemingly strong and sound business-strength scenario, have become far more pronounced than the markets have traditionally been used to. As a result, many market analysts are calling for 20-30% and more decline in the markets—far greater than might be expected in a normal economic business recovery.

Further compounding the new volatility in the financial markets is the global economy already discussed. This linking of money markets around the world adds a further layer of market reactions to world events; far more pronounced than ever before. The end result? While no one knows for certain, it seems obvious that the financial markets of the 1990s are more complex, volatile, unpredictable and fraught with a far greater propensity to react strongly and deeply to economic and political change. The implications for business will be interesting and important. This is clearly another case of perception of reality becoming reality. And, it would seem, a new paradigm shift in the "rules" of economics.

Chapter 2

Understanding Economics/ Business Indicators

Using Economics and Business Knowledge

The information in this section can be valuable if it is used systematically. There are a number of sources for the information listed, but here are some excellent ones that are readily available at any newsstand or local library.

- **"Forbes"**—This weekly business magazine will supply the types of economics information discussed in this section. It also provides well written articles on current happenings in companies in all industries, and analysis of business leaders and their strategies. So, it provides a good general picture of the health of the economy and specific industries.

- **"Business Week"**—Provides a weekly summary of events in American and world business. It presents all the business and economic indicators discussed in exactly the format used in this section. In addition, *Business Week* provides a preview of the various reports that are given each week and gives insight into how this data will impact the money markets.

- **"Fortune"**—This magazine is one of the oldest (begun in 1930), and certainly one of the most respected. It provides in-depth articles on companies in the news, business strategies

175

and leaders, the national and world economy, and personal investing advice. It is one of the better sources for understanding the long-term strategies of companies and industries.

- **"Wall Street Journal"**—the best known of the daily business news journals. It's loaded with economic and financial reports in its third section. The first section provides the day's business news, and the second section offers marketing analysis of company strategies and strategic directions in business. Most executives read the front-page *Journal* articles, since they tend to provide an interesting mix of news of the day with business strategies.

- **"Investor's Daily"**—is a more recent addition of the *Wall Street Journal* format. It also provides excellent daily, weekly, and monthly economic reviews and presents all the major indicators reviewed. It also attempts to combine current news with business and economic trends.

- **"Barron's"**—a weekly economic journal, *Barron's* provides the most comprehensive review of the stock, money, and bond markets. It also presents well researched, in-depth analyses of economic trends. Finally, the magazine profiles investors and financial analysts, providing helpful insights into market analysis.

The impact of the economy extends to automotive customers and has great impact on their attitudes and actions. First-time fix, and quality service, while always important, become a prime concern when people have to hold onto their vehicles longer and have less disposable income to put into service. Things like competitive interest rates on loans become extremely important in times of high inflation. (And GMAC's financial position can be of paramount importance to GM in recessionary times when it becomes the company's principal source of profit.)

The manufacturer's decisions involving capital expense and investment, and expansion/contraction of the business are directly rooted in the financial indicators and trends listed. Like all large companies, GM has the option of issuing stock (ownership equity in the company) and bonds (debt issues that yield high interest) to the public to finance its growth and investment. The value of these stock shares and the return on the bonds are among the most important issues facing the company and its shareholders. These things are directly proportional to the economic success and profitability of the company.

Monthly Economic Surveys and Reports

In addition to the leading economic indicators and money markets rates and data, there are a number of important indicators of economic activity and relative economic health released each week. These surveys and reports, in addition to reporting on the state of the markets, through their analysis can actually become day-to-day drivers of the financial markets. So, they are also trend predictors and have a great deal of impact on the short-term economy that stretches far beyond the specific conditions that each of the indexes is reporting.

These reports and surveys include:

— Personal Income
— Gross Domestic Product (GDP), which used to be referred to as Gross National Product
— Durable Goods Orders
— Federal Budget (Deficit/Surplus)
— Business Inventories
— Housing Starts
— Industrial Production
— Merchandise Trade Index
— National Association of Purchasing Managers (NAPM) Survey
— New Single Family Home Sales
— Factory Inventories
— Employment Levels.

Resources listed in this section, such as the *Wall Street Journal, Barron's Weekly*, or *Investor's Daily*, tell what reports and indexes will be released each week and each month. Watching these surveys carefully enables economists to predict short-term market movement very accurately. For auto manufacturer Wholesale people, this becomes an excellent "talking tool" when working with Dealers. The "Fortune Forecast" in each week's *Fortune* magazine provides an excellent analysis of all of these indicators and trends.

For an annual review of the direction of the economy, the **Fortune 500** published by *Fortune* magazine in April each year is an excellent tool. (*Forbes* also has an annual survey on this). This analysis of the 500 largest (in sales volume) publicly held firms in America each year tells:

1. The annual change in sales, profits, return-to-investors, and number of employes, performance statistics, of the top 500 companies.

2. Trends in sales from the base-year (1979 is the base year for 1993) through the current year.

3. Trends in profits from the base-year through the current year.

4. Productivity of the 500 in sales-per-employe from the base year through the current year.

5. Debt burden expressed as interest paid as a percentage of cash flow by the company.

These five areas give an excellent directional picture of the economy and the health of American business, particularly when the current year's Fortune 500 performance is compared to the previous year. This can be done both by company and by industry.

In addition to these trends and directions, the Fortune 500 evaluates each of the country's top businesses by total industry and by individual industry segment, i.e., "Motor Vehicles and Parts," for example, in terms of:

• **Sales**—in manufacturing and mining industries. There is a different annual ranking for service industries published in a special issue each year.

• **Profits**—net after taxes.

- **Assets**—at financial year-end.

- **Stockholder's Equity**—including capital stock, surplus, and retained earnings at year's end.

- **Earning-per-Share**—of common stock.

- **Total Return to Investors**—stock price appreciation over the year plus all annual dividend yield.

Here are brief definitions of the monthly economic surveys and reports indexes.

- **Personal Income**—the monthly income revenues paid to U.S. employes is tracked in conjunction with consumer spending. A rise in both indicators shows growing consumer confidence and a growing economy.

- **Gross Domestic Product**—the GDP is an indicator showing growth, decline, or stagnant state in domestic business production. Generally, a rise in GDP shows a growing economy in which there is increasing demand for investment capital, imports, and spending. This can be tempered by rising interest rates to control the growth and inflation tendency from a "hot" economy. It is one of the primary roles of the Federal Reserve Board to keep business growth, inflation and the general economy in balance.

- **Durable Goods Orders**—A rise in durable goods orders indicates increasing domestic economic activity, and a trend toward a healthy economy. When durable goods orders rise, production increases to meet growing demand, and business inventory backlog begins to grow. When inventories equal demand, production stabilizes. Growing inventories are a sign of slowing durable goods orders, and a weakening economy.

- **Federal Budget**—This indicator shows whether the operating budget of the federal government is running at surplus or deficit levels, i.e., whether the government is under- or over-spending its budget. The budget is currently running at record deficit levels in the $400 billion range. Balancing the budget and cutting spending should stimulate economic activity by lowering tax rates, stimulating investment, and lowering interest rates. Of course, this issue has been one of the most critical political issues in recent years as well.

This whole tax/revenue equation is an area now under great national debate, and one worth a digression to discuss. No matter what federal tax rates have been, in postwar America, tax revenues have gained at about 19.5% of our GDP. Based on history, raising taxes has not increased government revenues as a percentage of the economy. Over the past 44 years, there have been 25 changes in federal tax rates—from 28% to as high as 92% of top income levels. And, over this same period, federal government revenues as a percentage of GDP have consistently been about 19.5%. There is no demonstrated correlation between tax rate change and government revenues as a GDP percentage.

Also, in the postwar period, economic activity, or GDP, has accelerated in the four quarters following a lowering of tax rates, while GDP has declined in growth in the four quarters following tax raises. In the growth periods (after tax declines), economic activity, job creation, and the general markets strength have grown. So, it would seem that, since the 19.5% of GDP is a fixed value, 19.5% of a large, robust GDP is preferable to 19.5% of a small weak GDP.

- **Business Inventories**—held by manufacturers, retailers, and wholesalers, provide an indication of economic health through buying rates. Falling inventories normally indicate increased demand and increased spending and positive economic activity. Rising inventories show slowed consumption by consumers and businesses, and are accompanied by drops in production rates, signaling a slowing economy.

- **Housing Starts**—Construction is one of the most important economic indicators since it shows the willingness of people (individuals or businesses) to make their largest, longest term investments, and creates a very large number of jobs. Falling home mortgage rates also track rising construction jobs and loans. Autos, trucks, and housing, along with major commodities, are all vital key indicators of a long-term economic situation.

- **Industrial Production**—This indicator tracks output of the nation's mines, factories, and utilities. Growth in Industrial Production means raw materials are being produced, finished goods created, and power generated. Rising output reflects growing payrolls and a generally healthy economy.

- **Merchandise Trade Index**—This shows whether U.S. trade exports are leading (surplus) or trailing (deficit) imports. We currently are in a deficit situation, meaning we are spending more for foreign goods than other countries are spending for U.S. goods (with much of the variation depending on strength of the dollar versus foreign currency). A balanced trade picture is a key part of a healthy economy. Much debate exists about whether this imbalance is the result of unfair trade practices or of poor competitive performance.

- **NAPM Survey**—This is the monthly survey of corporate purchasing managers, regarding business activity trends. Rising activity in this survey is a leading-edge indicator of a growing economy, since a manufacturer's decisions to increase buying raw and finished goods must take place well in advance of production and consumption in the marketplace.

- **New Single Family Home Sales**—This is another indicator of both construction industry health and long-term consumer confidence.

- **Factory Inventories**—These compare production rates to consumption rates. Growth in inventories generally means lowered spending and a falling economy.

- **Employment**—This indicator shows farm and non-farm industrial payroll increase/decrease. It is the most direct and often quoted index of a strong or weak economic picture.

The general health of both the economy and business can be assessed accurately by using a number of economic activity, production, and industry-financial indicators. The specific groups are:

- **The Leading Indicators**—This group is the key to identifying trends in up/down economic activity; a group of seven measures that track what economists consider to be the key indicators of the direction of the economy, relative strength of business and the conditions of the stock and money markets.

- **Production Indicators**—This group of ten measures tracks the level of production of key strategic raw materials, power sources, and durable goods. They give a good indication of the level of manufacturing output.

- **Monthly Economic Indicators**—These track four measures of the economic picture to provide a picture of manufacturing activity and the relative level of the U.S. economy vs. the global picture.

- **Monetary Indicators**—These track the level of financial activity between the Federal Reserve Board, the national banking system, and U.S. business by watching four measures.

- **Money Market Rates**—These track interest rate levels in five areas to provide a guide to the attractiveness of commercial and private investment, which in turn provides insight into short-term (90-day) business development activity.

- **Foreign Exchange**—This provides the current exchange rates of key foreign currencies to the U.S. dollar. This information is vital in determining the attractiveness and balance of import/export activity between the U.S. and other countries, individually and in a global pattern.

- **Prices**—These provide price levels of seven key commodities. These move in consistent patterns with industrial production (equity) and industrial debt (bond) levels.

- **Real Estate Loans**—This indicator shows the level of lending activity in areas that track the housing markets and new construction, both major indicators of growth (or lack of it) of the economy. Note that new construction and first mortgages are usually more important indicators of economic health than mortgages on existing loans.

- **Industrial Production**—This is an index that demonstrates whether manufacturing plant activity is increasing or decreasing. It is tied to capacity ratings, which indicate what percentage of total U.S. plant capacity is being used.

- **Capacity Utilization**—This shows the average percentage of the country's ability to manufacture goods that is being utilized. Thinking of this as one plant that produces widgets, a capacity utilization of 75% means that it's producing 75% of its maximum widget production capacity. Generally speaking, a growing production capacity utilization is positive. In the case of the world automotive industry, however, there is extensive overcapacity, meaning the typical manufacturer has fewer customers available to him than the number of vehicles he can produce at 100% of all his manufacturing plants' output. This means, of course, that the automaker's investment in plants, tooling, personnel, etc., is basically greater than revenues can support. As this condition continues, plant closings, equipment liquidation, and employe cutbacks must occur to return the company to profitability.

  A parallel indicator to capacity utilization is productivity. This measure indicates how efficiently total available manpower is being used versus a 100% baseline reference. This is especially important to the American automotive industry as it works to lower its cost-per-unit, one important component of which is productivity.

- **Consumer and Producer Price Index**—This tracks the cost of goods and services to the consumer and of finished goods to the producer. These indexes are barometers of prices that are leading indicators of inflation. Increasing inflation tends to make the cost of borrowing greater, making it more difficult for individuals and businesses to purchase goods and invest in growth, slowing economic development and establishing a recessionary economic climate.

- **Gold Price**—This is an interesting indicator of the general strength of the stock and money markets. As stocks rise, gold will tend to fall and vice versa. So traditionally, investors will buy gold (and its sister precious metals) as a hedge against an inflationary economy and a weakening stock market.

Each of the indicator groups tracks the latest month's or week's market, money, or production values with those of the previous period, and the percentage of change for each indicator versus its value one year ago. Here are some examples of things to look for when using the indicators as tools to evaluate business and economic health.

- A rising ("Bullish") stock market that shows an upward trend indicates that businesses are generally increasing their value through investment, expansion, sales, and profit growth. Employment will be high, wages rising, retail sales strong, housing markets up, and the economy will be generally healthy.

- Bond yields, municipal, government, and corporate, that are growing indicate stable or lower bond prices. Since bonds are "debts," this indicates capital/stock growth and an upward trending economy.

- Increasing unemployment claims, especially when combined with increasing business failures, indicate a recessionary, weak economy.

- Production growth in raw materials and durable goods shows movement toward a robust economy. Activity in this area means growing production capability and inventories and indicates consumption is up and business strong.

- Imports that exceed exports combined with a growing budget deficit show the U.S. is in a debt position and is relatively weak vs. our trading partners. The deficit, which is currently at an all-time high, shows the country's debt level. It must be reduced for the economic health of the country, and to promote investment, the strengthening of our trading position, and the ability of the government to invest in the infrastructure and social programs.

Here are all of the measures tracked by the economic indexes.

1. **Production Indicators.** (These are put into an index with 1967 being the base year of 100.)
   a. Steel—in thousands of net tons.
   b. Autos—in units.
   c. Trucks—in units.
   d. Electric Power—in millions of kilowatt-hours.
   e. Crude-Oil Refining—in thousands of barrels/day.
   f. Coal—in thousands of net tons.
   g. Paperboard—in thousands of tons.
   h. Paper—in thousands of tons.
   i. Lumber—in millions of feet.
   j. Rail Freight—in billions of ton-miles.

2. **Leading Indicators** (These are also put into an index).
   a. Stock Prices—using the Standard and Poors 500 Index.
   b. Corporate Bond Yield—for Aaa and higher rated corporate bonds.
   c. Industrial Materials Prices—an index.
   d. Business Failures—the actual number of bankruptcy and Chapter 11 filings.
   e. Real Estate Loans—in billions of dollars.
   f. Money Supply, M2—in billions of dollars.
   g. Initial Claims, Unemployment—in thousands.

3. **Monthly Economic Indicators.**
   a. Industrial Production—an index.
   b. Capacity Utilization—percent of total available being utilized.
   c. Consumer Price Index
   d. Producer Price Index—finished goods.

4. **Monetary Indicators.**
   a. Money Supply, MI
   b. Banks' Business Loans
   c. Free Reserves
   d. Nonfinancial Commercial Paper.

5. **Money Market Rates.**
   a. Federal Finds
   b. Prime Rate
   c. Commercial Paper—3-month
   d. Eurodollar—3-month.

6. **Foreign Exchange.**
   a. Japanese Yen
   b. German Mark
   c. British Pound
   d. French Franc
   e. Canadian Dollar
   f. Swiss Franc
   g. Mexican Peso.

7. **Prices.**
   a. Gold
   b. Steel Scrap
   c. Foodstuffs
   d. Copper
   e. Aluminum
   f. Wheat
   g. Cotton.

Section IV   The Customer

Chapter 1

A Paradigm Shift in Priorities

We've referred to the automotive customer as "the most changed component in the industry." In this chapter, we'll see how this came about and what it means for today and for the future. Let's start by reviewing the "dynamics" for the business during the first 70 years, why it was a "manufacturing-driven" period, and what it meant to the customer.

For the first 70 years of its history, between 1903 (incorporation of Ford Motor Company and the acquisition of Buick and Oldsmobile by Durant) and 1973 (the date of the first OPEC Oil Crisis), the automotive business was in an extended period of positive growth and definition. This represented a very long "maturity cycle" for a manufacturing-based industry, and it was a period essentially supportive to the domestic Big Three: GM, Ford, and Chrysler. "Competition" during this period was more a function of capacity—production and distribution—than of competitive factors. For the largest segments of the market, choice was limited to the offerings of the three domestic manufacturers. So, as in any strong growth business, the share of each manufacturer became a direct function of what part of the growing demand their assembly plants and Dealer organizations could service, rather than what part they could capture through superior competitive attributes.

In this scenario, most of the important business variables of price, product features, availability of technology, etc., were controlled by manufacturers more than by competitive demands of the market. This allowed the domestic automotive companies to keep strong control over definition of the product, its service, and therefore, its costs.

The environment around the automobile industry, in addition to being free of serious foreign competitors or new domestics, was very friendly for the auto manufacturers in other key areas. As we've seen, fuel—the key variable in the "closed" domestic industry—was basically available and inexpensive. It was not a design-limiting factor (as it would become in the 1970s). There was little or no third party consumerism that had the political and economic clout of the organizations, i.e., the group led by consumer advocate Ralph Nader, that began to appear in the late 1960s. In spite of the depression during the 1930s, financial factors—inflation, interest, and taxes—were basically supportive of both manufacturer investment and customer purchase of durable goods like cars and trucks. Media and other electronic communications were far less hostile to big business than they have become since the seventies, applying far less pressure to big companies than they have today.

In this "incubator" environment, Alfred P. Sloan found the ideal situation to define modern segmentation marketing. With the Donaldson Brown "Standard Volume Plan," GM could break even at only 80% plant capacity. And since they had far stronger control over the variables of pricing and profit than today (remember, the company posted profits every year between 1920 and 1980), they could build a distribution strategy that would guarantee a 20% return-on-investment over each five-year cycle. With this range of control, backed by 60% of the industry's capacity, Sloan could focus on styling and status to drive strategies like the annual "new model announcement," often a cosmetic change that more or less allowed the company to increase prices while lowering costs through amortizing existing tooling and parts costs over longer periods, and through very stable labor costs (until the 1950s). Financing car and truck purchasing through GMAC's installment plans added even further to the corporation's high profitability. And in a market where GM-Ford-Chrysler set the standards and therefore defined quality and service, the companies could readily dictate just what "customer satisfaction" was.

In this "ideal" world of the first 70 years, Sloan's GM was able to move the automobile from Henry Ford's early "mass" definition—a good, cheap, serviceable car for everyone—to the segmentation pyramid's "mass-class" definition—a statement of the owner's socio-economic standing and a measure of social prestige.

As we've also seen in earlier chapters on the industry's history and economics, these conditions came to an abrupt and shocking (to the manufacturers and customers) end at about the time of the first OPEC Oil Crisis in 1973, although the Senate "Dealers' Day in Court" hearings of 1956, Nader's *Unsafe at Any Speed* of 1966, and VW's 380,000 Beetle sales in 1959 were all early warnings of what was to come. With the start of the "Politics of Oil" in the early 1970s and the arrival of the first Toyotas and Japanese Duals in (of all places) Detroit, the automotive business changed dramatically and forever. After 70 years of manufacturer control, there was a sudden paradigm shift in priorities:

- From very controlled to very intense competition.

- From fixed choice to a wide variety of offerings.

- From industry-controlled prices to competitively-driven prices.

- From easily available, inexpensive fuel to precious, volatile priced fuel.

- From manufacturer-defined standards of quality and performance to a true competitive range of offerings.

- From big, powerful, low-fuel economy cars to small, fuel-efficient, serviceable cars.

- From fast, powerful, fuel guzzlers to mandated low emissions, CAFE fuel-economy requirements.

- From manufacturer-defined levels of service and customer convenience to market demand levels of service and convenience.

And in all this change, the two most important factors to emerge were these: the industry now had, for the first time in its history, **real** choice to offer the customers in the bread-and-butter market segments. With this choice, although the domestic manufacturers didn't recognize it and were not ready to admit it, the business changed from manufacturer-driven/push marketing to market-driven/pull marketing. With this shift, the **customer** suddenly became the dominant factor in the industry, fully empowered through competitive choice!

Chapter 2

The Effects of Competition

High quality competition that, at least during the 1970s, responded faster to the changing environment than domestic manufacturers, caused some important changes in the business. These changes have virtually reshaped the industry extensively in the past 20 years.

The first of these redefined what an acceptable automobile or truck was. After the '73 Oil Crisis and the wave of consumerism and federal regulation that hit the industry at the same time, the new standards for the product were based on:

- **Quality**: Fit, finish, durability; how well things worked; how well panels aligned; even, smooth paint, free of imperfections; doors-trunks-hoods that closed smoothly, quietly and soundly; and cars and trucks that were more reliable than people had known before.

- **Fuel Economy**: The combined effects of OPEC, environmentalists and the government's CAFE regulations were requirements for each manufacturer's fleet to get far more miles-per-gallon than the vehicles of the 1950s and 60s, and to do it with much cleaner-burning fuel systems with carefully regulated exhaust emissions. The domestic industry had long held onto the maxim that you couldn't build a good, profitable, small car. But the Japanese proved you could, and in doing it, set a new standard.

- **Safety**: Government-regulated safety standards, crash worthy bumpers, rollover standards, brake system standards, etc., tracked right along with fuel economy and emission control requirements in the 1970s, and have continued since (although, a number of requirements were either frozen or relaxed during the Reagan Administration in the 1980s).

- **Price**: All of the requirements for vehicle improvements in safety, economy, emissions, and quality added significant, rapidly accelerating costs to building the product. In addition, the competitive factor put pressure on all manufacturers to differentiate more and faster with new technologies in fuel management, emissions control, braking, handling, and on-board customer conveniences. This added further research, development and new tooling costs to the product. As always, these costs were passed on to Dealers and customers. But unlike the earlier, pre-1970 period, the domestics were competing with foreign manufacturers that, at least during the 1970s and 1980s, could offer all these features at lower prices due to the relative strength of their currency (Yen and Deutschmark) versus the dollar.

Other impacts of the new competition included the emotional impact of instant communications through the rapidly developing electronic media. Another powerful force in media was the growing "tabloid mentality" of the 1980s. Large companies like GM pitted against the public, gave the tabloid press a major target for sensationalistic reporting that stressed drama and human interest and often "didn't let the facts get in the way of a good story."

On the economic front, Japanese and other offshore labor costs were significantly less per hour than the U.S. equivalent. Thirty years of "pattern labor contracts" in the industry, brought about by strong unions, had driven domestic labor costs to far higher levels than foreign competition. And the domestics' compensation package included costly benefits like health care, lucrative retirement programs, layoff pay and other perquisites that made our cost disadvantage even greater. The result of these impactors was that the American product, by the late 1970s, had become labeled as poor in quality and too expensive.

Another area coming under intense customer demand and media pressure was Dealer service. Just as the product had to compete against new competitive standards being set more and more by the buyer, so did the treatment and level of technical service the Dealer provided post-sale. And just as customers were demanding better products that performed to higher standards, they were also demanding better sales and service experiences with Dealers. Polite, honest sales people that acted like "transportation consultants" rather than the traditional high-pressure "car salesman" could be found at the import Dealer. Polite and honest treatment was also being demanded in the service department. And getting the car fixed right, the first time, and at a competitive price was becoming the new customer-standard requirement for the industry.

Customer satisfaction had long been an advertising strategy in the industry, with manufacturers promising to value the customer's business and care for him or her after the sale. Now it was a standard of performance that the customer demanded. The public was beginning to expect and demand the kind of consistent, no hassle, no surprise service they were used to getting in fast-food and motel franchises.

Driven by this trend, the "Customer Satisfaction Index" or CSi began to elevate to the level of an important standard for the industry. Each manufacturer had its own CSi process that looked at vehicle quality and at the quality of Dealer Sales and Service treatment of the customer. In addition, third party satisfaction surveys, the most influential of which was and continues to be, the J.D. Power survey, began to be one of the most powerful marketing voices in the industry. Whether or not CSi process was fair, and if or how it should be used in the franchise process became a new point of conflict between Dealers and manufacturers.

The end result of this intense new emphasis on the customer and customer satisfaction was this: as soon as a manufacturer stepped up to a challenge and delivered a higher level of customer treatment and service performance consistently, it became the standard for the industry. The luxury divisions of Toyota and Nissan, Lexus and Infiniti responded to the customer satisfaction challenge, and in short order were consistently at the top of the J.D. Power CSi ratings. In the process, they established a high standard for the entire industry.

And, as in the case of quality, their performance raised the entry level (or game ante—the "cost to compete") on customer satisfaction to the point that average industry performance improved greatly throughout the late 1970s and the 1980s.

Chapter 3

The Saturn Way

As we noted earlier in this text, one important positive outcome of the 1980s reorganization of GM was the emergence of Saturn Corporation. Saturn was meant to be a "Laboratory of Change" for discovering and refining new and better ways to conduct the business. And it was meant to explore every facet of the business: the design process, the manufacturing process, the union-management relationship, the Retailer process—virtually every aspect of marketing, design, engineering, manufacturing and retailing the automobile.

In each of these areas, Saturn was a great success. The product was of top quality, met customer requirements, and was competitively priced. The union and management developed new levels of cooperation and shared goals that resulted in consistently excellent quality. But perhaps most important, the Saturn Retailers (their term for "Dealers") evolved a whole new approach to customer care and treatment that has earned top customer satisfaction and fierce loyalty from their buyers. The "Saturn Way" proved so effective that, even when a major recall occurred—normally a customer satisfaction and public relations nightmare—it became one more way for Saturn to show their customers how highly valued they were. Setting up "painless" appointments and turning the recall into a major positive event, with barbecues and a "celebration atmosphere," demonstrated the real power of putting the customer first—**always.**

197

The success of the "Saturn Way," combined with the parallel success of the Japanese luxury products, had the same effect on customer satisfaction that significantly raising industry performance in quality had ten years earlier. It basically changed customer satisfaction from a competitive differentiator, a way to get a clear advantage over the competition, to an entry-level requirement—what GM (or any manufacturer) must do to simply stay in business and earn the right to compete.

In the process, Saturn created a new term, "customer enthusiasm," which describes the next level of competition in the customer-driven marketplace.

Chapter 4

Customer Enthusiasm—
The New Frontier of
Customer Satisfaction

The consistent level of customer support excellence established by Saturn, Lexus, and Infiniti have pushed the old concept of customer satisfaction to a new definition called "customer enthusiasm." Customer enthusiasm is an especially appropriate term, since it suggests going well beyond merely satisfying customers, to pleasing and delighting them, to ultimately turning them into enthusiastic advocates for the manufacturer. The idea of consistently exceeding the customer's needs and expectations gets at the core focus of delivering "customer enthusiasm."

Let's take a look at the characteristics of this new strategy, and see just what's required to be an industry leader in creating and sustaining customer enthusiasm.

Just as quality went from a major competitive differentiator to an "entry-level" requirement (a set of conditions an auto manufacturer must meet just to be in the marketplace) so has customer satisfaction. Satisfying the customer has become an absolute requirement just to be "allowed to compete." The differentiator in customer support and service is now who can do the best job of **consistently surpassing all** the customer's needs and expectations. Customer satisfaction, by definition, means responding to needs and problems, reacting well enough to satisfy a customer. Customer enthusiasm requires the automaker to have **proactive** knowledge of the customer's requirements. It's based on performance that will **prevent** problems from happening.

Customer enthusiasm means that the manufacturer and Retailer must **consistently exceed** customer expectations. So it requires systems that very accurately predict both what is important to the customer and trends that will lead to customer satisfaction. These two factors: proactive knowledge of customer requirements and the ability to identify trends that will lead to customer dissatisfaction **before** they do so are the starting points for customer enthusiasm leadership. Voice-of-the-customer, the Quality Function Deployment process that measures needs at every function in the product development and total ownership cycles, is the key to the first factor. Comprehensive, functional databases, with integrated expert systems that identify problem trends before they occur is the key to the second.

Creating enthusiasm goes beyond simply "meeting needs" to "delighting" the owner, creating positive surprises that customers are not used to experiencing. Saturn described this process using a term called "moments of truth" (originally used in the context of customer service by Jan Carlzon, Chairman of Scandinavian Air Service). Carlzon said that in any business, there are "50,000 moments of truth"—points of contact between company and customer which, depending upon how they are handled, will leave a lasting positive or negative impression on the customer. Top customer enthusiasm requires the business and its people to turn **all** these contacts, whether they're based on a problem, or are a regular contact or random communication between customer and employe, into rewarding, pleasurable "surprises."

The top priorities in customer enthusiasm building are capturing expectations and generating responses that are consistent and positive, and prioritizing them, providing the highest possible level of "hassle-free" service. The idea of "no hassle" service may be the single most important concept in successful customer enthusiasm. It sounds simple, and basically it is. But it also requires some thoughtful planning against a set of values. There are several basic guidelines:

1. Business processes must be designed for the **customer's convenience**—"external focus" and not internal.

2. Everyone who contacts and works with customers—retail and wholesale—must be **empowered, knowledgeable, and experienced** enough to assist the customer.

3. The vision, strategies, priorities, and especially the professional rewards system must **all focus on the customer** as the company's top priority.

4. The information management systems that support customer service must have **all the information needed to resolve problems** readily available and accurate.

5. All the systems and processes that service the customer's needs must be designed and administered based on **adding value**—quality, service, and superior utility—to the ownership experience.

6. Perhaps most important, the **purchase process must avoid the traditional hassle** associated with negotiating price, particularly adjusting trade-in value **vs.** new vehicle cost to a point that the customer is in an "upside-down deal" in which the trade-in value of the vehicle will never exceed the outstanding loan balance during the life of the contract. One-price or value-pricing is one way to accomplish this.

The customer assistance process should be based on the concept of **relationship building** between company (manufacturer and Retailer) and customer. In traditional customer satisfaction systems, the basic customer satisfaction relationship building tool was the survey—in automotive, the CSi Survey process. This concept is still vital, but it's not enough for customer enthusiasm. Survey processes also are **reactive**; they capture events after the fact. For "enthusiasm" we need to add activities that are proactive. One approach that has proven to work very well is the inbound/outbound 800-line system. In this process, customer assistance people make both proactive and reactive customer contacts. The idea is to establish a strong relationship with customers that not only responds quickly to solve problems, but establishes proactive lines of communication that measure requirements and identify trends before they become problems.

The "customer enthusiasm building" company works hard at **integrating functions**. It normally does this through teams that cut across functions to combine customer assistance, product technical expertise, and field contact experience. The idea is to focus as much expertise, knowledge, and as broad a range of expertise as possible to ensure that quality problem resolution is the standard.

An important objective of the customer enthusiasm strategy is building the highest possible level of **trust** between the customer and the manufacturer and Retailer. When the seller-buyer relationship achieves a level of consistent trust, the result is very high loyalty-retention of the buyer for future purchases. We'll examine just how important loyalty is in the next chapter.

For customer enthusiasm to be successful, the strategy to achieve it must focus on the **complete ownership cycle**. It must take into account every aspect of the owner's experience, from first awareness of the company and product, to the purchase decision, to the full use-experience of the product, to maintenance and repair experiences, to all communications with the Retailer and manufacturer, and finally to the repurchase decision. It must account for **all** events and interactions, leaving nothing to chance and minimizing the possibility of failure. Everything in the company's business process must be designed with the first priority of giving the customer a pleasurable, painless ownership experience.

Customer enthusiasm, when it reaches a consistent, high level of excellence, is an **advocacy strategy**. This means that the company's customers become its top advocates, replacing traditional advertising as the basic method of touting the company in the marketplace. Reaching the level of enthusiasm that produces customer advocacy means that all the requirements described above must come together, consistently, in the organization's culture and business strategies. Successful customer enthusiasm demands:

1. **Ready access** to decision makers for the customer, at the manufacturer and retailer levels.

2. Strict **accountability** with the organization for measuring, and responding to customers' expectations.

3. **Empowerment** to make decisions on customer problems, at

the retail and divisional levels, that cuts through layers of bureaucracy, without the second guessing typical of "old culture" automakers.

4. **Advocacy** for the customer that is best achieved through balanced teams that have representation for customer, product, Retailer, and the manufacturer.

The results of successful customer enthusiasm strategy in the new marketplace of the 1990s include:

- Top owner loyalty with highest possible owner retention.

- A stronger fixed operations (service and parts) base throughout the retail organization.

- The kind of marketplace strength that will sustain the company through the toughest economic times.

- And most important, **sustained profitable market-share**.

Chapter 5

The Importance of the Loyalty Strategy

We have talked about the critical importance of the loyalty strategy. Now we'll examine why it's so important. Landmark work in measuring the real value of "word-of-mouth advertising," the core of a successful loyalty strategy, was done by the TARP organization, a Washington D.C. consulting and research firm. Their work focused on assessing the real value of identifying and reaching out to unhappy customers as the basic approach in building owner loyalty. Here's what their research found regarding the "unhappy customer."

- Sixty percent of customers who have a problem won't complain. When these customers are asked why they don't bother to complain, their reasons are:
  — It "isn't worth the effort."
  — "Businesses aren't responsive anyway."
  — They don't know how to complain to the company.

In other words, they don't have much confidence that their complaints will be responded to, and there are no easy, available methods.

- Of the 60% of unhappy customers who don't complain, only 10% will repurchase the company's products or services; this represents only 6% of the company's total unhappy customer base that will repurchase.

- Of the 40% of customers who have problems and **do** complain, but **aren't** satisfied, 40% will repurchase. This represents 16% of the company's total unhappy customer base that will repurchase.

- Of this same 40% of unhappy customers who do complain, but **are** satisfied, the number repurchasing the product goes all the way up to 80%, or **32%** of the company's unhappy customers who will remain loyal customers.

- Unhappy customers who don't complain tell an average of 16 other people about their bad experience, while happy customers only tell an average of six people about their good experience. Since 32% of all buying influence comes from word-of-mouth references, the powerful impact of the unhappy customer becomes very apparent. And, the need to **find** and **help** the unhappy customer, and the value of positive word-of-mouth (vs. traditional mass media advertising) becomes obvious.

We know that the average business loses from 10 to 30% of its customer base each year, most often through problems customers don't complain about, followed by customers who complain, but are not satisfied. The influence of these "lost customers" is fully two-thirds of the 32% word-of-mouth influence on buying decisions. And we've seen that, while most of the lost customers won't bother to tell the company why they're leaving for a competitor's product, they **will** tell other customers and potential customers why (at about a three-to-one rate compared to happy customers who'll relate their good experiences).

We also know that replacing a lost customer with a new customer costs about **six times as much** as retaining the original customer. Another way of thinking about this is that the company's competition receives powerful advertising from the company's lost customers at only about one-sixth what the same influence would cost them through mass media advertising.

Chapter 6

Keys to a Successful Customer Strategy

Let's summarize this discussion on the growth in influence and empowerment of the customer, and of the vital importance of satisfying and retaining the company's customer base, by taking a quick look at a "baker's dozen" of the key elements of a successful customer strategy in the auto industry. Each of these keys will be reviewed in detail in the final chapter of this book.

1. Bring the **voice-of-the-customer** in continuous, consistent fashion to all the company's functions, business teams, and Retailers.

2. Make sure that all of the company's **products and services are properly aligned** with the customer's requirements, and that the brand images of the individual divisions reflect the needs and expectations of the division's target customers.

3. Ensure that the **quality of the business consulting given the Retailer** reflects the company's highest level of experience and expertise, and is based on a consistent business planning process.

4. Employ a **team-based advocacy process** in providing customer and Retailer assistance. Make sure the teams have representation (advocates) for the customer, product knowledge, the Retailer, and the division.

5. Take all the necessary steps to make the company a true **"learning organization."** This requires a continuous opportunity for a broad span of education and training, state-of-the-art information management systems networked across the complete organization, and a comprehensive competitive intelligence process.

6. Build and maintain an **external focus on the customer**, rather than an internal focus on the organization.

7. Establish an **executive-customer dialogue** process that features regular, structured top management contact with the customer population.

8. Establish a **relationship-based customer contact** process that uses both proactive (outbound calling process) and reactive (customer satisfaction measurement) initiatives.

9. Use **information that is predictive** through expert system application in databases with high functionality.

10. Focus on developing strong **retail employe enthusiasm** to attract, develop, and retain the best retail work force in the industry.

11. Ensure a **high degree of fiscal responsibility**, at retail and division levels, to be able to afford the resourcing needed to support customer enthusiasm.

12. Place the division's **top experience and expertise at the market place** working with the Retailer, and empower them to make decisions without "second-guessing."

13. Evaluate each element in the business process ("reengineering") to **ensure optimum value-added** to the customer and the Retailer.

Section V Aligning for the Future

Chapter 1

Organizational Change in the Service Society

We've seen the many sweeping waves of change that have characterized American business, society, and the economy over the past 90 years. This period has seen more significant progress and change than any other century in world history. And in a century of growth and change, the final decade, the 1990s, is seeing the most dynamic change of any period since the 1920s.

As in the 1920s, many factors are coming together to drive change. The United States has weathered a deep economic recession and has emerged in a position stronger than its Japanese and European competitors in its economic and business strategies in its key industries. And, perhaps most important, the distinct flexibility and diversity of the American culture is finally asserting itself. The result: as a nation we are responding faster and better to the new set of market demands for efficiency, productivity, quality, customer enthusiasm, and business reengineering than any global competitor.

This final section will examine this decade of change. We'll look at how organizations are changing in the "service society," organizations across **all** industries, manufacturing and service-based, including automotive. Then we'll focus on the automotive industry and take a look across the car and truck business in the early 1990s, at the new priorities and how manufacturers are responding. We'll examine the global auto industry as it stood at the end of 1993.

From there, we'll shift attention to two important people-oriented requirements for business leadership in the decade—the entrepreneurial attitude and teams—and at the things good teams do to succeed.

Next, we will examine a basic structural and strategic change in this decade that's taking place across **all** business—the move from "silo"—based functional hierarchies to cross-function teams.

We'll look at the "key indicators" that make success (or failure) in the industry, and at where General Motors stands—its "minuses" and "pluses" today. We'll look at a list of priority manufacturer "must do's" for the 1990s, the key success factors that will separate the winners from the "also rans." And we'll examine the reengineering process now underway across the industry.

From there, we'll analyze each key player in the industry—the customer/Dealer contact person, the Dealer, the customer and the manufacturer—what they will do and what they'll need, their absolute requirements.

Then, we'll examine the relative positions of the top global competitors—nations and manufacturers—and who (and why) the probable "winner" in the 21st century will be.

In the 1990s, an oxymoron has been crafted that perhaps better than anything else describes the direction of business: "Change is the Status Quo." The truth of this statement is inescapable. The only real constant we can see as we watch the business world in one of the most interesting periods in our history is **change**. Let's look at some of the hallmarks of this change.

- The highly vertically-integrated corporations that formed in the 20s and 30s, using Alfred Sloan's design principles of the "command-control" company, are becoming horizontally-oriented, "flatter and faster." All major companies across all industries are "reengineering" to improve responsiveness, quality, and profit.

- Separation between the customer and executive decision-maker is lessening, with the three-layered design being the ideal goal. In the customer-focused company of the 90s, the customer will never be more than one level from a top decision-maker and a "fast, fair" response to any problem with the company's goods or services.

- The span-of-control of managers and supervisors is increasing. Much of the work of the organization will be accomplished by cross-function teams rather than functional departments—the traditional isolated vertical "silos" of industry. Team make-up will reflect broad mixes of experience and expertise. This means that knowledge, information, and decision-making will cut across functions and be based on more in-depth understanding and ready access to all important information.

- True empowerment at the "market interface" is rapidly expanding to better understand and serve the customer. This places the ability to deploy resources, once the domain of top management only, with the customer contact person, basically "inverting the organizational pyramid."

- Manufacturing facilities will move from traditional assembly-line mass production to lean production and customer-focused mass customization, in which movable product assembly modules, served by a just-in-time parts process, will build products better and faster and to an individual customer's specifications and requirements. In the automobile industry, for example, traditional six-week to three-month waits will be replaced by two-week, and ultimately by three-to-seven day vehicle delivery cycles. (Toyota City is already producing custom products to a five-day standard for the domestic Japanese market.)

- The multi-layered "boxes" of the traditional vertical organization chart will be replaced by a structure featuring "floating circles" of teams and groupings of teams that interact with one another when and as needed. As the need for a team ends, it will "go away," to reappear as a new functional team when the need requires. This concept is known as the organic-dissipative organization. It brings empowerment, response, and high focus on customers and markets to replace the traditional command-control bureaucracy. In the evolving team-based organization structures of this decade, **trust** and **empowerment**—the ability of the team to make more knowledgeable decisions, to make them with the blessing and support of management, and not to be second-guessed—will be the final keys to success.

- The information-based, customer-service focused organization will replace and expand the traditional manufacturing environment. Knowledge will become the most important currency of industry. And the idea of delivering a product to a customer and then hoping that the customer (and others) will return to purchase again through a mass-media advertising approach, will be replaced by an "ownership-experience" based service philosophy. Word-of-mouth customer advocacy will be the top priority. This will require database driven 800-lines supported by the multi-discipline teams already mentioned. These teams will be geared to handle a broad-based range of customer requirements, from simple product/policy questions, financing, technical problems, clearing up vehicle operating confusion, the how/why of maintenance, to comparison with competitor products, pricing, etc. All this means that the knowledge base and information access of the manufacturer's customer contact person must continually grow.

- Continuing and expanding education for employes at **all** levels will become more of a required, job-integrated and fully company-funded process. As the lifespan of the technical knowledge-base contracts, and the knowledge requirements in the base expand, tuition reimbursement and direct education will be a must for attracting and keeping the best employes. More and more major corporations will develop company-based "universities" for continuing business, marketing and strategic education of all employes.

- Marketing will become more and more closely linked to service, or more precisely, to **customer** service. This is a logical result of database marketing replacing mass-marketing, and customer service replacing quality (which is becoming an entry-level requirement) as the top competitive differentiator. Being "close-to-the-customer," learning his or her needs and expectations, and translating those requirements into product and service specifications, is becoming the basis of sound marketing. Caring for the customer throughout the **complete ownership cycle**, from first awareness to repurchase, with the focus on retaining customers for future purchase, will be the top priority of the customer-focused decade.

To summarize, we can think of these change directions as 10 "reengineered" organizational characteristics:

1. The Horizontal Organization

2. Three Layers to Market

3. Broad Span of Control

4. Team-Based Decision-Making

5. Empowerment at the Front-Line (With the Customer)

6. Mass Customization

7. Organic-Dissipative Structure

8. Information-Based Organization

9. Integrated Education Process

10. Marketing/Service Linkage

These characteristics are rapidly becoming the priority points of focus for the successful 1990s business. And further, these characteristics are going beyond the automotive business world to become the hallmarks of the successful **organization** in any field of endeavor.

What will it take for a "good employe" to succeed in this evolving environment? Let's look at some personal success traits, things that will characterize the successful customer service employe in the winning company of the 1990s.

First of all, high potential employes will be entrepreneurs, people who have an "ownership mentality." And like all successful entrepreneurs, they will be innovative. They will be very action-oriented and will accept empowerment as a charge that is made up of equal parts of responsibility and authority. Each customer will be treated like a customer of the employe's **own** business who **must** be satisfied and retained if "their business" is going to succeed. (Later in this section, we'll examine in more detail the traits of the entrepreneurial mentality.)

The next characteristic of the successful employe in the 90s is to be **self-starting**. This is surprisingly important. Even very good employes in the traditional organization tend to wait for supervision to approve their actions and approach. And they spend much time reporting back on what they've done to make sure they really have management's support. The action-oriented "entrepreneur" designs an approach, takes the initiative, and quickly moves on to the next challenge. He is confident in his ability and experience, feels no need to "ask permission," and is very comfortable with having full charge of a situation along with a team of peers. For this to work, most traditional organizational cultures will have to change from being "risk-aversive" to supporting innovation and individual initiative.

Teamwork orientation is another personal trait that fits well with the changing 1990s organization. Team-oriented people have egos that are stimulated by the progress and success of their team. They are willing to subordinate personal gratification to support team victories. So, they're always open to the input and suggestions of others on the team. And they respect the knowledge and experience of their teammates. The team spirit value will replace individual "stars" in the 1990s.

By definition, in a changing world of changing technologies, **education is a top priority**. This means that the best employes will be characterized by a thirst for learning and knowledge. Computer science, database management, customer-service techniques, team-based management, automotive technology, and marketing strategy, are just some of the areas where customer service professionals will have to work very hard, often on their own initiative, to stay on top of their field. The educational process will have to include equal parts of tuition reimbursement at the college level, function-specific business programs, and internal company-sponsored training. Company-supported "university" curricula will become standard in a decade characterized by "learning organizations."

Customer focus will have to be far more than a slogan to the customer service employe professional of the 1990s. They will have to know enough about their products and services, their Dealers, and their customers' requirements to be able to **think** like the customer or the Dealer. In-depth employe knowledge, supported by technical and Dealer-support teammates, will have to be continually focused on responding to the customer, and responding to the Dealer. An important element of the customer services job will be continuing education in the techniques of customer service, in the operation and service of the company's vehicles and products, and in the policies and procedures of the organization.

Another aspect of successful customer service will involve maintaining an **external customer focus** balanced by an integrated internal and external perspective. The internal piece means working closely with the team to build a combination of rapport and a know-ledge base that reflects an equal balance of the technical, Dealer, customer, and marketplace experience of the team. Keeping on top of current product problems and conditions, making sure the contact person is up-to-date on warranty trends, policy and procedures, and knowing what Dealers are concerned about (including the economic climate and sales and service picture) are all part of the internal half of the balanced perspective. The external perspective starts with understanding customer and Dealer requirements—a balance of technical knowledge and empathy for the customer. It also includes building the understanding of the employe's business, the competition and key factors like economic change and the customer service process.

Without question, maintaining "**computer literacy**" is a basic requirement of success. But this extends beyond understanding basic program software operation. It also means understanding database technology and the database marketing process. In fact, understanding the differences between mass and database marketing implies other areas in which the customer service professional will want to become proficient.

First, understanding the role of **customer services as a basic driver in marketing** is most important. The key to understanding customer/competitors, and to forming a solid competitive intelligence system is found by continuously tapping into customer requirements and customer experience. What better way to develop an understand-ing of the marketplace and its priorities than through a continuous, systematic interaction with the buyers of products **and** services and those of competitors. And the same logic applies to the Dealer organization. Organizing the input from these audiences into marketing databases, by subject, i.e., pricing, product preferences, performance options, service-abilities, dealership preferred services, areas of technical misunderstanding and problems, desired conveniences, etc., is the first step. Then, matrixing these marketing subjects vs. demographics, geographies, etc., can be the best possible reference tool in building marketing plans, advertising campaigns and promotions. This all means that the customer and Dealer contact persons will be very important "cogs in the marketing wheel" of the 1990s.

Staying current on product operation, service features, and technical problem trend items are priorities for top flight customer services contact personnel. Not only will this promote responsiveness to the customer and Dealer, it will also provide an improved source of product information for engineering and manufacturing. This also enhances the credibility of the Manufacturer's Marketing Division with the customer and the Dealers as well. More than ever before, the basic currency of business is **knowledge**, knowledge of the product, the customer, the Dealer, policy and procedure, data management systems, the principles of customer service, and the role of customer service in both the quality process and the marketing process.

The synchronous process, originally a manufacturing technology system, has become as important to customer service as to assembly plant work management.

Organizing the internal and external service process around the ownership experience is much like designing a synchronous engineering and production strategy. The customer services team, with its customer, Dealer, and technical assistance elements, must be fully synchronized to perform in a responsive manner with the engineering, manufacturing, delivery, maintenance and service systems. Communication between each element must be timely and clear; feedback must be used to improve the product and service support of the product. And the entire process must be synchronously managed better than the competition! This is an absolutely key element of marketing success.

Finally, success in the automotive (and in practically any manufacturing/service) business in the 1990s will require replacing traditional "company politics" with **a team-based ethic**. This means old practices like avoiding risk, assigning blame, asking permission, fear of reprisal, and protecting the status quo, will have to be replaced by true empowerment, cooperation, two-way communication, knowledge base development, and even the freedom to fail-and-learn. The reason is simple. The competition is too intense for an organization that wants profitable market-share to be anything but the highest quality, the most responsive, and the most efficient supplier. Productivity, quality, and customer response must come together in equal measure. Reward and recognition, therefore, will have to be based on pure, objective, superior performance.

All of these traits will be necessary to be successful in the 1990s in what we might call the "Keiretsu Teams" of customer services. Why Keiretsu? In Japanese culture and business, a keiretsu is a "semi-formal" organization of groups or companies that are not organizationally aligned, but, are aligned to serve one another in a well-defined and symbiotic way for a given process.

They are symbiotic because each partner of the group or the successful organization serves each other, as well as themselves, to a precisely defined level of expertise or materials production. If we look at the automotive business specifically, a keiretsu is a traditional, long-term alliance between an automaker, parts suppliers, materials suppliers, banks, and even nonrelated business partners. Each of the partners has a guaranteed amount of parts or materials to deliver, financing to supply, transportation of materials and products to contribute, design work to contribute, etc. So, for our purposes, the term "keiretsu" implies symbiotic teamwork—where each team member must be present with experience and knowledge, be committed to a common goal like pieces in a puzzle, and have a well-defined and guaranteed role in the team's activity if the team is to succeed.

Each team member must bring unique knowledge and experience—of customers, Dealers, and products—to the process. And most important, each partner must work with other team members in a true spirit of cooperation to be successful. Finally, to be truly empowered, the customer services team must be **self-starting**, willing to take on responsibility and authority without "asking permission" to get the job done. In a word, the team and its members must be **entrepreneurial**.

Let's take a look at process management and results management and their proper relationship. The process for each function in customer service is most important. It must be synchronous, efficient, have the right process measures, and represent the best possible use of the organization's resources. It should be laid out using process model(s) and carefully checked to make sure that it meets all the above criteria. But remember, the "input" to the process model consists of the customer's requirements, and the "output" is based on satisfying the customer. Finally, the "loop" is closed around the process model by measures and feedback; since the measures must reflect the customer's satisfaction, it follows that the process measures and results measures must both be based upon the satisfaction of internal and external customers. Therefore, all system measures should be evaluated on this basis—do they deliver added-value to the customer?

Chapter 2

Across the Industry in the Early 1990s

As the automotive industry entered the 1990s, all the major global manufacturers were faced with a number of common challenges. Global recession and massive overcapacity were taking their toll on Toyota and Volkswagen as well as on GM, Ford and Chrysler. In the U.S., Boards of Directors began making their presence felt as Fortune 500 companies responded slowly to cost-cutting challenges. GM was one of the first to feel the trend, seeing their top executive team replaced in the most dramatic shake-up since Durant's replacement by Dupont and Sloan in 1920. Toyota and Volkswagen were undergoing similar secession changes. These were the major "dynamics" of change:

- The industry began rapid downsizing, worldwide, in response to overcapacity and cost-management pressures.

- Every manufacturer in every industry, not just automotive, wrestled with culture change as traditional internally-focused organizations tried to respond to customer-driven markets.

- There was a general movement toward the horizontal, broad-span of control, market-focused organizational structure, and

221

away from the traditional vertical command-control structure introduced by GM in the 1920s. The traditional design, perfect for the manufacturing-driven environment, was simply no longer viable in the competitive, fast-response marketplace of the 1990s.

- Cost-cutting movements in every automotive manufacturing business included: plant closings, de-emphasis on robotics-based automation, deep labor cuts, aggressive cost-control initiatives with suppliers, management changes, and reassessment of non-core investments. In short, each automotive manufacturer was rapidly getting serious and more focused in the new marketing environment.

- Each manufacturer began serious evaluation of their parts and components groups with an eye to increasing responsiveness, becoming more cost-competitive to gain price advantage, and investigating expanding their markets outside their respective companies. The aftermarket parts and components markets offered great opportunities if only the automakers could overcome internal cost and structural problems that made them slower and more expensive than the independent suppliers like NAPA. And meeting this challenge posed more than a marketing problem to the domestic automakers. Customer satisfaction, **the** core goal, was **very** strongly impacted by the cost and availability of parts. The first automaker who could find the formula for "doing it right" would gain a vital marketing edge.

- Dualing and the rapid influx of foreign Dealers made the Dealer Network Strategy a top-priority issue. In GM, with its many old-line Dealers entrenched in metropolitan markets that were rapidly shifting to new-suburban population centers, the problem was especially important. Tough issues had to be dealt with: positioning of dealerships in shifting markets; downsizing to remove small-volume, unprofitable points and refocus on newly-defined major markets; exclusivity requirements that manufacturers had to demand from Dealers to recapture lost brand equity and serve customers' unique needs; educating Dealers and employes in new business planning, customer support and technical areas; and manufacturers fighting to recapture brand images diluted by multiple-line dualing patterns.

In product development, each manufacturer had to step up to requirements that impacted cost-of-manufacturing and owner cost-of-operation, environmental concerns, safety, and new levels of owner convenience. These issues included:

— Fuel efficiency

— Alternative power plants that offered enhanced performance, efficiency, and cleaner emissions with emphasis on dual overhead-cam technology

— Tire and suspension technology that included computerized traction-control

— Weight (materials) reduction without loss of crash worthiness

— Further electronic fuel, suspension, and steering controls

— On-board sound and communications systems

— Powertrain efficiency, exploring new areas like energy-storage flywheels

— Continuously-variable transmissions

— Safety concerns, including ABS, dual air bags, high-impact frames, bodies and bumpers as standard items

— Enhanced serviceability and longer maintenance intervals

— Battery technology development (nickel-iron, zinc, and chlorine approaches)

— Route-guidance systems that can factor in traffic flow.

Finally, the combined impacts of government regulation, environmental concerns, and safety have had deep and lasting impacts in the industry. These impacts include cost containment and negative influence on public opinion at a time when owner loyalty and emotional support for the domestic industry is more important than ever before in the history of the business. In this complex and difficult market, several key strategic factors occurred. First, the deep recession and political upheaval in Japan have forced Japanese product prices upward and forced their industry to temporarily abandon their global market-share strategy (10% of the world market by 2000) in favor of focusing on profitability. At the same time, the global economic downturn of 1989-1992 put great pressures on the major economic powers to begin to solidify trade markets. The result has seen the consolidation of markets and resources in the European Economic Community, the North American Free Trade Association and early movement toward an Asian Consortium, with each market controlling from 400 to 600 million consumers. The following two charts summarize the global picture in the second half of 1993.

Global Picture Today

- World economy in slow recovery; Industry improving financially, strategically; U.S. sales up 8.5%.
- Pent-up demand; Leasing are keys.
- Industry the focus of major trade blocks.
- U.S. at 33.6% world share.
- Truck growth strengthens further; Class 8 up strongly in U.S.
- U.S. gains 8 of Top-10 sales positions.
- Chrysler sales Up 20% in 93; To 13+ of industry in U.S.
- GM at 31.5%; Ford at 24.2% of domestic industry.
- Asia (Japan, Korea) at 38.5% of world share.
- Europe at 27.9% of world share.
- Japan down 2.7% (recession, government).
- MITI pressures Toyota to support Honda, Nissan.
- Japanese refocus from share to profit.
- Accord, Camry retain their Top-3 positions in sales in spite of Japanese recession, political problems.
- U.S. industry mounting strong surge in quality, technology, and customer focus.
- All manufacturers, worldwide, reengineering to improve costs, responsiveness.
- U.S. production Up 6%.
- Chrysler low-cost domestic producer; lowest cycle-time in new product development.
- Ford integrating U.S./European design, engineering.
- Europe (Fiat, VW) entering lean production.
- Toyota, BMW; Early leaders in the process of mass customization.
- VW behind in quality; manufacturing technology.
- Trend to watch; Yen down 10% in late 1993.

World's Top Manufacturers		
1.	GM	7.1 Million Units
2.	Ford	5.8
3.	Toyota	4.2
4.	VW	3.5
5.	Nissan	3.0
6.	Volvo-Renault[1]	2.3
7.	Chrysler	2.2
8.	Peugeot	2.1
9.	Honda	1.9
10.	Mitsubishi	1.8
11.	Fiat	1.8
12.	Suzuki	1.4
13.	Mazda	1.2
14.	Daihatsu	.8
15.	Hyundai	.7
16.	VAZ	.7
17.	Fuji	.6
18.	BMW	.6
19.	Daimler Benz	.5
20.	Kia	.5
	Isuzu	.5

[1] With the failure of the Volvo-Renault merger, these two manufacturers fell out of the top 10.

The Entrepreneur

We noted the importance of the entrepreneurial spirit in developing a successful customer-focused company. The key to the entrepreneurial spirit is for each employe to truly feel like an owner. Winning companies will have as many "owners" as they have employes. And each employe will take the performance of their company—the **entire** company—personally. Here are 20 traits that all successful entrepreneurs share.

1. An entrepreneur "signs his own check." He truly feels like the company's success rests with him.

2. An entrepreneur is as empowered as resources allow. He can make decisions bound only by the company's resources.

3. An entrepreneur takes things that impact the business "personally." Anything that happens in any part of the company happens to the entrepreneurial employe.

4. An entrepreneur thinks of fellow workers as teammates rather than bosses or rivals.

5. An entrepreneur has empathy for each function of the business.

6. An entrepreneur pays attention to competitors.

7. An entrepreneur thinks beyond just meeting measures to how his performance impacts the customers.

8. An entrepreneur feels responsible for the "bottom-line."

9. An entrepreneur thrives on work and responsibility.

10. An entrepreneur is honestly aware of his performance; no one else has to tell him.

11. An entrepreneur is goal-oriented.

12. An entrepreneur understands his organization's S-W-O-T (Strengths-Weaknesses-Opportunities-Threats) profile.

13. An entrepreneur is involved beyond job description requirements.

14. An entrepreneur understands customer needs.

15. An entrepreneur takes it upon himself to learn.

16. An entrepreneur has a "volunteer" mentality.

17. An entrepreneur never says "It's not my job."

18. An entrepreneur seeks out responsibility.

19. An entrepreneur is governed by goals, not the clock.

20. An entrepreneur knows his organization's history niche; has great pride in it, and understands its strategic direction.

From "Silos" to Cross-Function Teams

Traditionally, business, including automotive and virtually all industries, has formed around **functions**; things like finance, personnel, engineering, marketing, sales and service in an "organizational hierarchy." These structures then evolved into the vertical, silo-based bureaucracies that are common across all industries. Over time, these disciplines have become deeply entrenched and internally-focused. They have, in most cases, become separate business entities, isolated from one another and, as a result, "bottlenecks" in the business process of the organization.

The primary goal in businesses that evolved this way in manufacturing-driven, under-capacity markets has become the protection of the "silos" and the bureaucracy they created. This has been, more than any other factor, how "turfism" and the obsessive focus on span-of-control by each "silo" function have developed as the predominant features of the business culture. The characteristics of the vertical "silo"-based company include:

- The silos will protect and expand upon operating budgets from year to year. This concept puts a premium on spending all of the current year's budget to justify an operating budget as large (or greater) the following year. This is done principally through maintaining current programs and adding new "programs" that the function is responsible for developing and managing. In the automobile business, these annual programs often become part of the Dealer's subscription or purchase program, ultimately adding additional cost (and questionable value) to retailing a vehicle.

- The silos, over time, will increase the number of people managed and the span-of-control the function is responsible for. This is the basis for the "turfism," creating and protecting the size of organization—or the turf—that a function controls. It is also a principal cause of the development of different goals and business agendas, that often conflict, between silos.

- Just as the silos will expand and protect the size of their organization, they also protect all the resources the function controls—its people, operating budgets, facilities, property, equipment, and (more recently) its information management systems and databases. (Over the past two decades this has led to great proliferation and redundancy in the number of information databases in GM. And it has led to extreme overlap and redundancy in the information collection and storage process. The result has been a kind of information gridlock that ties up people and systems, adds complexity instead of clarity to understanding issues, and slows response to the customer.)

- A common practice in this vertical culture is "showcasing" silo managers and key people. This often happens at the expense of other organizational functions and business units. The result is almost always increased isolation of functions, and the creation of different goals and working agendas—and always, more internal focus. The business goals become the expectations of the managers rather than the expectations and requirements of the customers.

- People in a silo learn to shield the function's top managers from "bad news." In the process, people quickly develop a risk-aversive attitude characterized by extreme reluctance to take any chances or to launch any meaningful change if there is any possibility that a new initiative could fail. In the old culture, waiting for competitors to try new concepts, and trying nothing new that could fail and thus hurt one's career path, are the business norms.

- The most damaging result of this organizational "silo behavior" is a lack of innovation and leadership in technology and marketing. Traditional silo cultures seldom create the paradigm shifts that change the fundamental rules and directions of the business.

- Silo-based organizations develop highly bureaucratic structures with many, many layers of management and multiple reviews and approvals for any decision. All of which created very slow cycle times (the time from input-to-output), poor response to markets and customers, and costly, inefficient business processes. In the auto industry, the end-result was a cost-per-unit of domestic products much higher than the competition's. (A trend that today, fortunately, is being reversed).

In total, the vertical "silos" business structure became a **very** internally-focused organization. And it was an organization that became, over time, far more concerned with perpetuating and "growing" itself than with listening to its customers, benchmarking its competition, or "inventing" better ways of doing business and adding value to its products and processes.

We've already made the point that the successful business of the 1990s and beyond, automotive, or **any** manufacturing or service business, will have to abandon the silo culture. They will have to move from this slow, unresponsive, self-serving, internally-focused vertical structure to a "flatter, faster, more responsive" business concept. The key to the successful horizontal organization will be overlaying the cross-function teams concept over the traditional silos.

To be successful, **cross-function teams** will have to have certain characteristics:

- They will have to have representatives of each function (or silo) on each team. For example, a cross-function team working on developing or supporting a new product or business process might well have members from design, engineering, manufacturing, sales, service, human resources and financial silos.

- They will have to be strongly linked to key suppliers and (in automotive) Dealers. Including suppliers and Dealers very early in the development process, so they have well defined roles and responsibilities, is one of the keys to the "lean enterprise"—a complete channel-to-market built around just-in-time and continuous improvement.

- They will have to be truly empowered to make decisions (and held accountable for their decisions) **without** seeking permission of their separate silos. In other words, the team goals and not the silo goals must prevail. And, they will have to be able to control and deploy the resources necessary to implement their decisions.

- They will have to contain a **balance** of expertise, experience, and advocacy for different points of view—in automotive, for the product, manufacturer, Dealer, and customer perspectives. This will ensure that the necessary information and expertise is always available at the point of decision making without the slow and costly "meetings and memos" method prevalent in today's business environment.

In other words, the cross-function teams will have to have the resources, knowledge, and control to function as independent strategic business units. This means they will have operational missions, their own strategies, goals and action plans in the business planning process.

Instead of building around functions, the business teams will have to structure themselves around product-lines and the support processes for those products. This means that each team will have to maintain an continuous linkage to the voice-of-the-customer. They will have to be able to continually tap into customer, Dealer, and supplier inputs that are fixed parts of the team's business process and not "after-thoughts."

To make voice-of-the-customer a consistent work-driver, the cross-function teams will need performance standards and measures that accurately reflect the customer voice. And the rewards and recognition process that supports team members must be based on team members' performance against these customer-driven standards. Perhaps most important, organizational managers will have to remove the traditional barriers to innovation. Managers will have to communicate **and** demonstrate that innovation and intelligent risk-taking is desirable; the stipulation being that mistakes are "OK" as long as people learn from their mistakes and use them as tools to create positive change.

This area, the willingness to accept errors as part of the learning process, and encouraging people to take chances that are sure to produce some failures, will be one of the most difficult (and most necessary) changes in the automotive business culture. To work, constructive risk-taking will have to be built into the human resources management process and supported by a rewards system that recognizes positive risk-taking as a desirable management trait. All organizations capable of producing paradigm shifts in their industry are supportive of innovation and of people who are advocates of change.

Where does this cross-function teams concept leave the traditional functions, the "silos"? Will they have an organizational role in the new business structure of the 1990s? Absolutely. The functional silos will become the "learning centers" of the new organization. In this new role, the silos will have two principal functions:

1. **To build databases of knowledge** for their functional disciplines; staying in tune with state-of-the-art changes in technology and process, maintaining a historical library of the discipline and the company's competitors, maintaining information databases, carrying out competitive intelligence and

benchmarking their functional areas within and across industries.

2. **To create the performance standards** for their functional areas. The cross-function process teams will then use these standards as guidelines and measures in product and process development.

How might career progression work in the new-structure, cross-function team based organization? Basically, people would rotate between service on teams and time spent in the functional areas (replacing the old-culture approach of rotating between jobs in the functions).

While members of cross-function process teams, people will be actively and directly involved in conducting their company's business—planning, designing, marketing, selling and servicing its products. During their tenure in the functional organization (the "silo"), people will focus on upgrading their skills and knowledge; on learning about their industry and competitors, and on developing the standards of performance for their functional discipline.

The traditional "silos" then, instead of being isolated operations contesting with other functional areas for turf and control, will become the resource centers for the "learning organization." The job of the silos in the future organization will be to replace their internally-focused bureaucracy with a dynamic educational and performance measurement base for the organization.

Now let's examine the specific kinds of behavior and activities of successful business teams.

Things Teams Do To Succeed

Another "performance standard" for winning in the 1990s is the team-based organization. Just as entrepreneurs have certain "traits," teams that are successful have certain things that they **do consistently**. Here are the most important.

1. Set standards for decisions.

2. Ensure balanced advocacy—for the product, the customer, the company, and the Dealer.

3. Demand facts; use logic to make decisions.

4. Use a process model to organize facts, look at possibilities, examine consequences and the impact on **all** the people involved.

5. Create real impact, that is, total cost **and** worth analysis.

6. Use protocols that neutralize separate agendas, in other words, the good of the customer and the company comes before any individual function or department.

7. Apply synchronous principles.

8. Balance skills, experience, and technical expertise.

9. Commit to persevere; "pay the dues" that extend beyond the job description, or the eight-hour workday.

10. Control their working environment.

11. Earn credibility in their organization.

12. Ensure mutual respect for all members of the team and their knowledge and points-of-view.

13. Listen to teammates' positions.

14. Understand teammates' styles, preferences and priorities.

15. Have empathy for teammates, customer, and all constituents.

16. Build negotiation skills.

17. Allow direct customer impact.

18. Reach decisions that support the company Vision.

19. Keep an open-mind; avoid pre-conceived ideas.

20. Be fully prepared.

21. Understand competitors and competitive differentiators.

22. Understand **all** customer requirements.

23. Know how their decisions represent voice-of-the-customer.

24. Focus on building owner loyalty; positive word-of-mouth.

25. Analyze what competitors do in similar cases.

Key Indicators for the Business

In this incredibly tough global market, two critical priorities have emerged. First, marketing in the auto industry has been clearly redefined from a "push" to a "pull" based strategy. This means that product design, distribution, and customer services are now being defined in the marketplace, by the customer, and can no longer be driven by the manufacturer. As GM reengineers, this scenario places perhaps **the** top priority on retail business planning as the proper method to:

- Determine product allocation through Dealer forecasts

- Monitor voice-of-the-customer

- Improve retail operations management

- Deploy resources

- Develop advertising and merchandising strategies

- Define training and education requirements

- Improve communication between Dealers and Divisions, and within the dealership

- Shape the winning customer satisfaction strategy.

This last point, customer satisfaction and the development of industry-best customer services is the **most** important priority of the new market-driven auto industry of the 1990s. Customer services in the **broadest sense**, from owner awareness, through purchase and throughout the complete ownership experience to the repurchase decision, has become the most important strategic competitive factor in the automotive marketplace of the 1990s. Customer service has become as much a part of the winning automaker's strategy as products. The advent of inbound/outbound 800 lines, the Saturn concept of Customer Enthusiasm, and Chrysler Corporation's "Customer One" strategy, are all clear indicators of the importance of the **customer** as the definer and driver of industry performance.

Notice that Saturn has defined its customer strategy as "customer enthusiasm." It is most important to understand that this is not just a play on words, and that customer **enthusiasm** is not the same as customer satisfaction. Customer satisfaction means **responding** to the customer and satisfying the customer's requirements. It is basically a **reaction** strategy. Customer **enthusiasm**, on the other hand, is a proactive concept. It demands that the manufacturer understand all the customer's requirements beforehand, and then consistently **exceed** those requirements. The result must be to delight the customer with **pleasant** surprises at each potential "moment of truth." Customer satisfaction, like quality a few years ago, has become an entry-level requirement. Customer Enthusiasm has now become **the** competitive differentiator.

Today's Scenario

Given the changes in the automotive business in the past 20 years, since the first OPEC oil crisis in 1973, and the look we have taken at positioning in the global market today, the next step is to evaluate GM's position in the marketplace of 1993 in terms of its principal weaknesses ("minuses") and strengths ("pluses"). These "minuses" and "pluses" of today's GM are summarized in the following charts.

GM Minuses

- Devaluation of "paper" (GMAC Bonds) (although this is currently improving with the resurgence of GM Stock).

- Conflicting Dealer and company goals (share **vs.** profit). Dealers need constant cash flow and monthly profit, while the company needs to rebuild its market share for the long term.

- Number of models; platforms. Basically, there are too many and they are not well aligned with needs segments as compared with many competitive offerings.

- Loss of traditional image-alignment. The "cradle-to-grave" strategy that gave each GM division ownership of a specific set of socio-economic customer targets has been blurred and largely lost.

- Weak capital position (< $7 Billion as of early 1993).

- Lack of profit in North American Vehicle Operations.

- Market-share at 30% - 35%.

- "Expensive" labor contract; betting on productivity gains to overcome higher fixed costs.

- Entrenched bureaucracy; still quite vertical. (The reengineering process is pushing the company toward a horizontal, business team focus.)

- Parts operation responsiveness; cost and availability.

- Non-core business costs. (On the plus side, these areas are generating consistent revenues and profit.)

- Dealer Network "Modernization" demand.

- Unit-cost disadvantage ($500 - $1,400).

- Supplier relations strained.

GM Pluses

- Saturn's redefinition of process in GM

  Customer Enthusiasm

  Synchronous

  Union Relations

  Selling Process

  Word-of-Mouth

  Loyalty Focus

  CSi; achieving top position in a low-cost product where performance can't be "bought."

- NAAO Strategy Board (vs. Management Committees)

- Reduce model count by 8 (of 62); platforms must go from 12 to 5.

- Streamlined decision-making process.

- Engines; "underskin electronics/technology."

- North American Purchasing initiative.

- Focus on Retail; pull-back from fleet/subsidies.

- Customer-focus in the evolving GM Vision.

- Downsizing and refocus on the GM core business.

- Culture change/reengineering initiatives underway throughout the corporation, operations and marketing divisions.

- The move toward common processes and business systems, designed to eliminate redundancy, improve response, lower costs and achieve consistent performance.

- Powerful new databases are nearing implementation that will make proactive product distribution possible, moving GM much closer to true "pull" marketing driven by voice-of-the-customer.

Manufacturer "Must Do's" for the 1990s

If the preceding discussion represents today's marketplace scenario in the automotive business, what will the winners have to do to separate themselves from the "also-rans" in the coming decade? This section summarizes the key "must do" strategies for the 1990s. Any GM reengineering initiative, if it is to be successful, must account for these priorities.

1. Align **Vision-Strategy—Organization Structure** to direct reengineering.

2. Base Vision-Strategy on **Customer Loyalty**; win customer advocacy. Accomplish this by being the most responsive to customers and markets, and being the **best** at reading voice-of-the-customer.

3. Develop a **Customer Empathy** culture.

4. Establish a **Customer Dialogue** Process; do this through regular executive interaction with customers on a marketing level (**but not** to replace established process resolve individual customer problems).

5. Develop a **horizontal organization with front-line empowerment**; cross-functional teams.

6. Gain control of **all elements of cost-per-unit**.

7. Use the **right measures**; cost containment, customer requirements, responsiveness, cycle-times, organizational alignment, alignment of products and services. All measures must directly reflect value-added for customer and Dealer.

8. Focus on **long-term strategic investment** over short-term dividend yield. (This will require further work by Boards of Directors.)

9. Focus on **continuous improvement**, not "pass-fail." (Ironically, to get to an environment that supports innovation and

enables paradigm shift breakthroughs, a culture that supports continuous, incremental change must also be in place.)

10. Develop **superior customer enthusiasm**; be the best at understanding expectations and delivering requirements consistently. Develop a Trust-Credibility strategy that focuses on developing customer belief in and support of the GM Divisions.

11. Drive **profitability** through share, cost-control, and superior customer services.

12. Build a true **union-management partnership**; in which pay and perqs are based on performance. There must be common goals and rewards based on a common business plan. Manufacturing and Marketing must be involved in labor negotiations.

13. Make the **best use of information, knowledge**. This should include a **competitive intelligence** process and the growth of GM as a "learning organization."

14. Replace mass media advertising with **earned trust and database marketing.**

15. Establish **superior Dealer partnerships** through shared goals. These goals must be mutually focused on achieving owner **loyalty**.

16. Develop a **Dealer Network** featuring the right numbers, in the right locations, "business plan-linked" to the Manufacturer, continually trained on common systems, properly capitalized, and conforming to standards.

17. Establish education and retraining, a **GM/Divisional University** process that offers a wholesale/retail "Masters" degree program.

18. Balance **warranty/customer satisfaction**, a clear understanding that sound warranty management **supports** customer satisfaction.

19. Return to **Cradle-to-Grave**, to align with turbulent, complex, segmented markets. This must include a product strategy that recreates traditional and newly conceived image alignments of divisions and market segments and a support process that matches the image, recreating an image of GM as a "mass-class" manufacturer.

20. Build leadership in the **Mass Customization** revolution, an absolute focus on lower cycle-times and on the ability to profitably meet a customer's precise requirements better and faster than the competition.

21. **Integrate key suppliers** into a GM "vertical strategy" in Keiretsu-like fashion.

22. Focus on a **public relations effort** to positively reshape the institutional image of the company into a more customer-friendly, open, and progressive orientation.

23. **Fix the parts problem**; make parts available, competitively priced, and expand the commercial market for GM parts and components.

24. **Leverage GM's technology leadership** through highly visible marketing and advertising initiatives.

25. Focus on the **GM "people resource,"** particularly through business-creativity teams.

26. Employ **synchronous principles** throughout all Operations, Staffs, Production, and Marketing functions.

27. Focus on **pull-marketing**, becoming marketing-driven in all aspects of design, production, and distribution of GM products and services.

Process Reengineering in the Auto Industry

Within the marketing divisions of General Motors, and of the other domestic manufacturers, there are a number of business processes that are designed to support the retail network and provide added value to the customers and Dealers, all in support of the vehicle ownership experience. Let's look at the most important of these business processes **as they work in the industry today.**

1. **Information Management.** Collecting, organizing and disbursing information from retail networks, and other sources that capture data describing the performance of the industry in sales, service, customer satisfaction, etc. The requests for this information come from many different sources—marketing divisions, the corporate staffs, NAO, etc.—and its use serves many different purposes, many of which can be redundant and have little bearing or value-added for customer or Retailer.

2. **Retail Business Planning.** The process of analyzing an individual Dealer's market, dealership performance, strengths, weaknesses, and opportunities, and using it to develop sales forecasts and business and communication development action plans. The Retail Business Planning process is in use in similar (but different) formats in most GM Divisions (it should be a common process). Today, it offers the Retailer business development value, but is not a viable tool for serious forecasting and product-marketing planning.

3. **Warranty Claims Process.** The complete management of the warranty system, driven by retail submission of warranty claims and the financial reimbursement of Dealers filing the claims, to keep customers' vehicles operational and enable Dealers to provide the labor and parts necessary to support the process. It includes information management, accruals determination, profiling, claims processing, and the Retail auditing process. Good Retailers use it as an important driver in their business planning, particularly in inventory management, training, and customer satisfaction analysis.

4. **Sales Forecasting and Allocation Process.** Projecting the market requirements for volumes of each product, driving the production process to manufacture and deliver the products, and deciding how to allocate those products across the retail distribution networks. Traditionally, this has been an internally-focused process that uses past performance and capacity utilization requirements ("push") to drive plant production and distribution of product to market.

5. **Retailer Allocation/Distribution Process.** Using the "turn and earn" system to flow products through the retail distribution network based on Dealers' past selling performance.

6. **Retail Selling Process.** Management of customers through the ownership cycle, from awareness through the repurchase decision by means of the sales consultant process in the dealership. This has also traditionally been an internally-focused process. Its purpose has been to liquidate inventory rather than to align product attributes and cost with customer requirements.

7. **Retail Training Process.** The process for identifying needs and delivering training to meet those needs in areas including business management, sales, product, technical service, parts, customer satisfaction, finance and insurance, rental and leasing, business planning, marketing, advertising, and other retail skills areas. In the traditional concept, training delivery has flowered through two primary channels: the GM Training Centers which focus heavily on product servicing and diagnosis, new product orientation, and generic retail skills areas; and in-dealership "package" training managed by each marketing division, focused on technical, business and customer topics of current interest.

8. **Retail Network Process.** Planning, franchising and managing the process of placing Dealers in retail operations and ensuring compliance with the sales and service agreement that governs the business relationship between manufacturer and retailer. While there are central rules for governing the manufacturer-retail business process, each marketing division

has its own retail network management operation for its own product brand distribution system.

9. **ADI Marketing and Advertising.** The processes for developing and implementing geographically-based marketing strategies and the advertising strategies to support them, including advertising agency management and the retail ad process. This process combines the development of core strategies and promotions, supported by shows and exhibits, with the retail-managed brand advertising process.

10. **Retail Service and Parts Process.** Management of the equipment, facilities, parts inventories, training, and fixed operations process that supports the warranty, maintenance, diagnosis and repair of the customers' vehicles in the retail network. This includes technical assistance, wholesale field support for Retailers, field service engineering, and service information functions (like service manuals and bulletins publication).

11. **Customer Assistance Process.** The complete customer communications and problem resolution process, including the 800-line manufacturer support process, the retail support process, field wholesale support, mediation and arbitration—all the efforts in the system designed to respond to customers with questions or complaints.

12. **Program Development Process.** A management system for identifying, designing, approving, and administrating programs for retail and wholesale development, marketing, and customer satisfaction. Input to this process comes from every area of the business, including internal (division-corporate), Retail, and customer sources.

The reengineering process that is taking place across the industry (and across nearly all business industries) today is meant to optimize these processes and ensure that they deliver the highest possible added value to the customer and retail network. Basically, reengineering analyzes business processes for strengths, weaknesses and opportunities for improvement, and then redesigns the processes to realize these opportunities.

There are really two parts to reengineering. The first is to make sure that the business processes and systems in use are the **right** ones for doing the job to the highest possible value with minimal waste, redundancy, and lost time. This addresses the **effectiveness** issue— that what's being done to run the business is what **should** be done, and represents the best possible use of the organization's resources. The second part of reengineering addresses the **efficiency** issue—are the processes that are there being executed as responsively and as accurately as possible. This gets at external-focus, fast cycle-times, quality of delivery, and the value of the product that each process delivers.

If we reexamine the list of business processes from the first criteria—effectiveness—here are some important observations that can be made:

1. **Retail Business Planning** should be the "umbrella" process for the rest. Done properly, it will become the driver for forecasting, resource allocation, retail training, inventories management, communications, information flow, and virtually all the other process areas. For this to work, the manufacturer's contact person who works directly with Retailers must have high levels of experience, expertise and empowerment; the Retailer must be given in-depth training in the process; and the retail plan must form the basis of the "wholesale contact agenda."

2. **Sales Forecasting and Allocation** and the retail allocation and distribution process, given a reliable retail business plan forecasting process, and strong, expert wholesale support of the Dealer's in-plan development, would be driven by the retail planning process. The most important ingredient in this mix is a **fully** empowered, highly experienced and skilled wholesale contact that works with the Dealer at a much higher management level than is typical of the system today. Instead of being the traditional "entry-level" position, this scenario would make the Dealer contact role a high-middle management job that would likely take 10 years or more experience and top performance to qualify for.

3. **Information Management** could also be driven through the retail planning process. Support information **for** Dealers and requests for information **from** Dealers should be a product of the business plan and support of the plan. It's important to eliminate redundant requests, and request for information that do not yield relatively direct information back to the Dealer and customers.

4. **Marketing and Advertising** would, in the ideal environment, be closely connected to the planning process. Ideally, the marketing strategy should provide the "connection" between manufacturer planning and Dealer planning. And, to move from traditional "push" marketing to "pull" marketing, in which the customer drives the distribution strategy, this link will, ultimately, have to be made. This, again, demands a retail planning process that gathers accurate, reliable information continuously, that can be used with a high reliability factor in the distribution and marketing planning process.

5. **Retailer Training and Network Development** should also be driven by the retail plan. If the retail business plan were to become the core "agenda" for communications between manufacturer and retail network, the plan would be the method for identifying training needs, ensuring these needs are met, and "customizing" the training based on the specific requirements of each Dealer in the system.

6. **Warranty Management** would become the central "trigger" in the information management and decision-making process, directly controlling database updates, parts inventory management, customer satisfaction trends identification and Dealer needs identification. This will require fully integrating the warranty management databases with the other information systems that track products, customers, Dealers, parts, and revenues. And it will require the overlay of an intelligent system that continuously interrogates the warranty database to identify trends in product problems, expenses, and customer expectations.

7. **Program development** would become a systems output of all the above functions. And it would be much more "custom-tailored" to the needs of the individual Dealer and responsive than the cumbersome approach that is in use today. A single cross-function support team could manage this.

Overall, there could be fewer business processes if they were organized from "customer-in," starting with retail business planning as the core discipline. Next, to get at the "efficiency" issue for business process reengineering, here are some observations and suggestions regarding streamlining and adding value to the processes as they work in the industry today.

- Nearly all the current business processes, due to the internal ("push") focus that they were developed under originally in the manufacturing-driven/undercapacity growth environment, have become "reversed" over time. They are driven by the manufacturer and not the customer. And, in most cases, there are several layers of costly review/approval cycles that take place before end-users have any opportunity to impact the process.

- This makes the process slow and complex and adds many unnecessary layers of review and approval. It also breeds a tendency for different "silos" to compete with one another in trying to manage and control processes based on different goals and business agendas.

- One of the main results of this situation is weak "outside-in" (customer to company) communication. It also causes generally slow cycle times. And it adds to the expense and resources-drain that comes with slower process cycles. It also assumes that the organization is a suitable substitute for the customer in terms of making value judgments about products and support processes.

- To get to pull-marketing, the key issue is **reversing these processes**, virtually turning them around 180° so that customers and Dealers input and initiate and the organization executes according to these market inputs. This would also be the key (and probably the only way) to productively change the culture that created these processes.

- All of today's business processes are "silo-driven." To move to the cross-function teams (discussed in this section), it is absolutely necessary to change to customer/Dealer-driven business process. Most of the layers in the industry bureaucracy today come from internally-focused and push-driven business processes. And much of the "turfism" that has developed over time has been a direct result of the vertical silos protecting their direct interests and span-of-control in the process.

- As a general rule, business processes should be:

    — Driven by continual customer input.

    — Implemented by cross-function teams.

    — Designed so that "silo" functions provide the knowledge base and standards of performance.

    — **Not** be budget-driven, in terms of the traditional practice of justifying programs.

    — Designed to separate customers from decisions by no more than one call, three organizational layers, and 72 hours (a key "cycle times" issue).

    — "Lean enterprise" structured, with the company and suppliers aligned in a manner that ensures just-in-time delivery and no waste of time, money, systems, or facilities. This involves entrusting suppliers with design and implementation roles well beyond the traditional concept, and requires a business partnership driven by common goals.

Managing the Customer Experience

Managing the customer experience better than the competition does is the key to profitable market-share in the automotive business. When the "customer management" (meaning positive support and **not** manipulation) process is working as efficiently and effectively as possible, the Sales and Service functions play vital and well-defined roles in the process.

The Sales Organization's role should be built around a customer target population consisting of first-time buyers and existing owners of competitors' products—the "conquest" (won away from competitors) target. This means that Sales must marshall marketing intelligence, advertising strategy, and Retailer support all focused on gaining the attention of prospects at the point of awareness and intention to purchase—the front-end of the ownership life cycle. Their responsibility is presenting the product in its best light—as a competitively superior offering—based on their knowledge of customer requirements and a product-process package that meets all requirements; superior product design, features and benefits; and price that reflects best value-added for the money with the least "hassle" (as discussed earlier in the "Customer" section). This also means that the Sales function has to pay close attention to the "placement" marketing process; the distribution of the right products to the right markets when they are in demand.

Gaining the prospect's attention; positioning and pricing products in a competitively superior manner; managing the retail sales consulting process (remember, based on **meeting the customer's expectations**); through vehicle order placement—these activities must all be directed by the Sales (and associated Marketing) functions. So **incremental market share**; first time and conquest customers "belong" to the Sales organization.

Once the vehicle order is placed, the customer ownership responsibility transitions to the Service organization during the delivery process, which is jointly owned by Sales and Service. The balance of the ownership experience—through the warranty and post-warranty (or "customer-pay" service cycles) periods becomes the responsibility of the manufacturer's Service organization. This means that the customer retention—keeping the customer for the second sale and beyond—is the purview of the Service department.

In terms of marketing goals then, Service owns "loyalty"—the percent of owners who repurchase the company's products **and services**. This is a logical "fit" since Service controls the maintenance, serviceability, diagnosis and repairs, and parts support processes that make up the customer contact elements of the ownership experience; the things that ultimately will determine how well the original "sales promise" was met. And, to close the loop, the information databases that Service manages—warranty, customer, and vehicle data—become tools to transition the process back to Sales when it's time to close the repurchase.

In this scenario, while Sales and Service functions each have defined "customer ownership" marketing roles, **each** has the shared role of building customer enthusiasm (which, as you'll remember, is "delighting the customer," the next level of customer satisfaction). In the traditional automotive organization, customer satisfaction was pretty well defined as the responsibility of Service. In the 1990s customer-focused company, **everyone** has this responsibility. This was proven by the experience of Scandinavian Air Service as documented by its CEO Jan Carlzon in his book *Moments of Truth*. And, as we've seen, Saturn has been a leader (along with Toyota —Lexus and Nissan—Infiniti) in making it an axiom in the auto business as well. In fact, this responsibility for serving the customer goes well beyond the marketing divisions (Sales, Service, advertising and distribution), and has equal ownership in the design, engineering, and manufacturing communities as well.

Next, we'll look at what each "player"—the wholesale contact person, the Dealer, the customer and manufacturer—"needs" to pull the 1990s organization together for optimum performance.

What Each "Player" Needs

Each of the "key players" in the automobile industry has certain important needs and expectations, requirements that must be met consistently, for the business to be successful. By "key players," we mean the manufacturer's contact people who work with Dealers and customers, the Dealers themselves, the customer, of course, and the manufacturer. These "needs" can be either requirements that the player needs to **receive** from the other players in the scenario, or **performance** that the player (contact, Dealer, manufacturer) must deliver to the customer. The first part of this discussion summarizes the most important of these needs, requirements, and performances for the manufacturer's customer/Dealer contact person.

1. The Manufacturer's Customer/Dealer Contact Person

- **Must know company procedures and policy.** The contact person must have a clear understanding of the priorities and standards by which decisions should be made. In situations where these priorities and the interest of a customer are in conflict, they must know the level of their empowerment to decide.

- **Must be a front-line "customer satisfier."** The contact person must be empowered to handle as many cases as possible without referring to management. However, they must feel free to call on their teammates for information and counsel. It's vital that all the facts and important information be known and that the best technical expertise be called on to reach decisions that are fair, and that can help correct the **source** of problems.

- **Must balance expense management (short-term goal) and customer/Dealer satisfaction (long-term goal).** The contact people are the stewards of the company's financial resources. But, at the same time, they are also the advocates of the customer and Dealer. One of their important roles is to properly balance these two interests in a way that protects both stakeholder (stockholders **and** customers) and strategic interests. The proper balance will combine fiscal responsibility with a priority on doing everything that can be done to satisfy the customer and develop a positive image as a customer-focused company.

- **Must have excellent interpersonal skills.** The successful contact is an excellent communicator who knows how to deal with anger, confusion, frustration, and how to turn these negative emotions into positives.

- **Must be able to deal with a great deal of abuse/anger without "taking it personally."** The contact person must always work from the basic assumption that a customer's or Dealer's anger is about a problem, and not with the contact person. This takes equal measures of maturity, empathy, and empowerment to do what's necessary to respond to problems.

- **Must also help build high Dealer Satisfaction (DSi).** The Dealer Satisfaction Index (DSi) is the measure of how satisfied a Dealer is with the support received from the manufacturer. A knowledgeable, empowered Dealer phone contact that is accessible and understands the Dealer's business is a sure prescription for satisfied Dealers. And a strong customer assistance operation further supports Dealer satisfaction by providing a backup that can help Dealers as well as customers.

- **Must help manage the Division's expenses by analyzing problems and recommending solutions.** The contact person's decisions should be based on a logical, analytical process rather than a "blank check" approach. Finding the root causes of problems is of greater value to customers than "throwing money" at problems without finding and correcting the source causes.

- **Must serve as the customer's and Dealer's advocate** in a very balanced way. Must be able to balance policy, procedures and priorities with the customer's/Dealer's interests. And, they should understand each involved person's position and needs.

- **Must be consistent in decisions.** This is especially important in working with Dealers, who have a right to expert fairness and consistency in the process of resolving a customer's problem.

- **Must be fair and willing to give the customer the benefit of the doubt.** The contact person should start from a basic assumption that the customer is telling the truth as the customer knows it.

- **Must understand how to cope with anger**, both their **own** anger and that of the customer or Dealer. One of their most important contact skills is knowing how to neutralize anger and turn it into rational thinking.

- **Must have good negotiation skills**, knowing how to leverage information, policy, trade-offs and options. This often means giving a customer or Dealer less than they ask, but enough to satisfy.

- **Must be able to use the vehicle-customer-Dealer databases** as diagnostic tools to help Dealers identify problem sources. Two of the most important steps in problem analysis are framing the issue and gathering the information necessary to make a good judgment. The customer/vehicle databases and the customer and Technical Assistance Center (TAC) case files are two of the most important tools in accomplishing this.

- **Must be familiar with Dealer's CSi performance**, and be able to analyze why there are weaknesses and how to improve them. Again, information is the contact person's most important tool. Divisional Dealer information systems can be a major help in analyzing a Dealer's CSi performance. And customer assistance, technical assistance and field contact, working together as a team are the best ways to perform this analysis effectively.

- **Must be familiar with the Dealer's Warranty Management performance.** Every Dealer has patterns in managing warranty. A good manufacturer contact person makes it a priority to know them.

- **Must understand how to review a Dealer's Operating Report** to find weaknesses, deficiencies, and probable causes. An in-depth knowledge of the Operating Report and how to analyze it is an absolute must for a successful Service/Sales contact person. The Retail Business Plan process is the proper format to work with Dealers to improve their operations performance.

2. The Dealer

- **Transaction cost.** This is the cost to the Dealer to retail a unit. It must reflect full value-added and add no unnecessary cost to the unit that the Dealer cannot recoup. This is the key to profitable market-share.

- **Respect and recognition** from the manufacturer, particularly those who contact the Dealer to assist in business matters.

- **A true business partnership** in which the manufacturer considers the Dealer as an equal with common needs and objectives. This is also one of the principal roles of the Dealer Business Planning process.

- **Responsiveness.** When Dealers have questions or problems, an immediate response with specific answers to their questions from the manufacturer is crucial.

- **Attentive listening**—the sense that when they have a concern or problem, there is someone who'll pay complete attention and will represent them fairly.

- **A knowledgeable counselor**—wholesale contact people who understand the business and the product and who can supply them with fast and accurate responses.

- **A voice in the business** so the Dealers can express their front-line knowledge of products and customers in a way that will improve performance in both areas.

- **Competitive products**—cars and trucks that excel in all areas of design and performance, and with competitive pricing and financing.

- **Fair and even-handed treatment**—a sense that they will be given the benefit of the doubt and treated as important business assets by the manufacturer.

- **A polite attitude.** The Dealer does not want to be treated with a confrontational attitude. The key to this is to always remember that the Dealer and division really have shared goals and must be business partners for balanced success.

- **A sense of teamwork with the manufacturer.** Dealers want the manufacturer to recognize that they have common concerns and objectives.

- **Policies and warranties that are competitive with the industry's best.** Part of the value of the franchise lies in policies and practices that provide the Dealer with as much protection as possible.

- **Product distribution based on market demands.** This is a function of strong business planning with Dealer/manufacturer input. It means product allocation and forecasting based on sound market analysis. And it is the core to a "pull" marketing strategy.

- **Products of top quality and the "serviceabilities."** The Dealer wants to know that the products he sells can be serviced consistently within specification, and will satisfy the customer.

- **Database marketing**—an approach that uses expert systems in information databases as a way of aligning specific Dealers and customers without much of the expense of mass media. This is a key factor in building owner retention.

- **Benchmark Customer Support Systems.** GM needs to have an umbrella of customer support services that are clearly the industry's best.

- **Customer advocacy.** Each Dealer must have, on staff, a person empowered to act in the customer's interest at the management level. (This is an important part of the Customer Response Process discussed earlier in this text.)

- **Top quality service training.** One of the Dealer's most important needs is to have Technicians who can diagnose, repair, overhaul, and service the products he sells. The training supplied by the manufacturer is the key to this requirement. A strong retail employe benefits package with compensation, benefits, and long-term job security is equally important.

- **Timely and accurate service support**—a combination of Technical Assistance (TAC), the in-dealership contact, publications, and training.

- **Responsive parts support.** All the Dealer's best efforts to serve the customer can be undone if he can't get parts for needed repairs in a timely (24-hour) fashion. This is a combination of a good inventory and a responsive parts organization.

- **Reasonable answers for the customer.** The Dealer wants to be able to count on the manufacturer to support him in responding to the customer.

- **Honest responses**—an obvious need, and one that "works both ways."

- **Use of artificial intelligence as a business tool.** GM must implement business-operating systems in which expert systems make trend predictions that pre-empt changes in the business and in markets.

- **Facilities** that support the brand image of the division, and that represent industry leadership in customer convenience and appeal.

- **Strategic location.** GM Dealers must be located in the best locations in key markets.

- **Knowledge of competitors.** Part of the Dealer Business Planning process involves "comp-shops" (competitive comparisons) of competitor Dealers to learn their strengths and weaknesses. This process is a key part of Dealer Business Planning. All Dealers should do this.

- **Available financing**—basically, a line-of-credit at a reasonable rate that exceeds average receivables, typically over a 90-day period.

- **Realistic performance standards** for Dealers that address volumes, productivity, financial performance, customer satisfaction and personnel development.

- **A manufacturer that "walks the talk" of customer satisfaction.** The manufacturer's decisions should consistently support the customer satisfaction priority.

- **Most of all—consistency** in decision-making that is based upon knowledge, a sense of fairness, and a desire to build the business partnership and the value of the franchise.

3. The Customer

- **Competitive excellence in vehicle styling and performance**—a car or truck that exceeds the popularity and perceived brand image of the competition.

- **A top quality, highly serviceable product** with maintenance that offers the least inconvenience and a product that "doesn't break."

- **An honest, reliable Dealer**—a feeling that they're getting the best deal, without hassle. And if they need service or repair, confidence that only what's needed will be done, will be done right the first time, and (if not covered by warranty) at a fair price.

- **An honest, reliable manufacturer** who delivers a vehicle that represents top value for the dollar, and who will stand behind the vehicle throughout its life cycle.

- **Competitive warranties and policies.** The warranty coverage should be at least as good as the competition, and the manufacturer should consistently stand behind it. The manufacturer should be fair about out-of-warranty conditions.

- **Service that is fast and reliable**—a lube-oil-filter service in less than 30 minutes and basic service the same day. If ordered parts are involved, two-day service is the expectation.

- **Conveniences that make the service experience hassle-free** Free or low-cost loaners or alternate transportation, a comfortable, well-equipped lounge area, ease of payment methods, a smooth, quick write-up process—all the things designed to minimize the inconvenience of service.

- **Listening and response from manufacturer and Dealer.** First-call response is the ideal. Customers want an answer to their question or a solution to their problems in a reasonable amount of time.

- **Promises that are kept.** When a Dealer or the manufacturer offers a fix, it should be done, done right, and done quickly.

- **Professional support** including technicians who can fix the product, Service Advisors who can carry out solid questioning and write-up, salespeople who don't "play games" or put them in upside-down deals, and a responsive manufacturer.

- **A sense of empathy and care** on the part of the Dealer and the company; attitudes, response and customer services that demonstrate the manufacturer's and Dealer's customer focus.

- **A sense of urgency that reflects an understanding of the size of the customer's investment.** The car or truck is still the second biggest purchase customers make. They expect the Dealer and manufacturer to recognize that and act accordingly.

- **Honest dealing**—a process that prevents the customer from entering an "upside-down" contract in which owner equity never exceeds outstanding loan. This also includes full disclosure and honesty in the ordering process.

- **Safest possible transportation**—cars and trucks that reflect state-of-the-art safety features and are built as well or better than any competitors products.

- **Manufacturer and Dealer that fully stand behind the product.** Most customers feel, as we've seen, that the warranty should cover the vehicle's lifetime. Worst case, the customer wants the manufacturer/Dealer to share in the cost of repair for serious out-of-warranty conditions.

- **Treatment that is polite, positive, and not defensive.** Again, this goes back to the size of the investment, and the general mistrust in which customers hold Dealers. This is an absolute key in turning this historical distrust around.

- **Uninterrupted transportation.** The absolute necessity of transportation for the two-car/truck family in today's society demands products that work consistently and a dealership that provides access to alternate transportation when they don't.

- **Cooperation between the parties who supply the product and its service.** No customer wants to get caught in the middle in a dispute between manufacturer and Dealer.

- **Knowledgeable "Transportation Council"**—a Dealer who can help them select the **right** product to meet their needs, and at a price and financing structure they can afford.

- **Access to Dealer/Manufacturer** during non-business hours when it is convenient for the customers, and at any time they need help.

- **Convenient location**—Dealers that are easily accessible from the customer's home/work, particularly for servicing.

- **"One-Stop Resolution"**—the ability to solve a problem with one phone call/visit to an empowered person.

- **Dialogue with the manufacturer**—ways to easily express

their requirements, requests, problems, questions with someone who can give them the right answers and **act**.

- **Warranties that match usage.** Customers would like to be able to select the type and extent of vehicle warranty to best meet their needs.

- A **"Voice at the Management Table"**—another way of expressing the need to have someone listen who can and will help.

- **The ability to fix whatever might occur to the product**—a commitment by the Dealer and factory to have well-trained Technicians in place.

- **A polite, respectful attitude.** All customers have the right to be treated respectfully, responsively, politely, and with an attitude of genuine concern.

- **A sense of helpfulness.** Customers want to feel that when they approach the Dealer (or manufacturer) with a problem, everything possible will be done to help them.

- **A "friend" and not an adversary.** The Dealer and factory should have the same objectives as the customer—quality products that are fully protected, convenient to operate, and basically trouble-free.

- **Consistency** in decision-making with **no surprises**.

- **Honest Dealers who are knowledgeable and participate in managing their business**. The time for adversarial roles between factory and Dealer has passed. Collaborative effort between the parties has reached the status of entry-level for success. Each Dealer must be a committed, full-time business manager.

- **A positive customer attitude by the Dealer.** Dealers must understand that the customer is the number one business priority, and that understanding and meeting customer require-ments is the **only** path to profit.

- **A positive customer attitude by the divisional contact person.** Empowerment has been given to the contact; it must be combined with customer-focus; an understanding that the satisfied, repeat customer is the **absolute** key to the company's success.

4. The Manufacturer

- **A responsive parts process.** A 24-hour delivery is becoming far more of a competitive "must have" than a good thing to do. Failure in parts support can bring down the rest of the system. Both availability **and** price are keys. And the parts organization must have customer enthusiasm as its top business priority.

- **Well-trained retail technicians, sales people, and service advisors.** With customer requirements as the top priority, having the best front-line retail sales and service people is the most important support process, right along with world-class products.

- **Customers who maintain their vehicles.** Today's products, with more complex computerized on-board systems than ever before, while far more trouble-free, also demand proper maintenance—for the good of customer and company.

- **Owner retention**—loyalty repurchase rate that consistently exceeds 75%.

- **Well-trained and knowledgeable contact people.** Without question, the factory's front-line contact people must consistently be the best performers on the wholesale side. They need the broadest array of knowledge and skills in the business today. And they must be senior managers who are fully empowered.

- **Union contracts that reflect a partnership.** A clear understanding by both union and management that competitive prices and top quality products are to everyone's benefit.

- **Product development cycles of 24 months or less.** From concept to production, GM must get back to and set new world class levels.

- **Product production cycles of two weeks** from order entry to delivery to customer.

- **A horizontal, team-based organization** that features lean, responsive performance.

- **Marketing technology that reduces mass media cost**—the application of database marketing to directly align customers and Dealers.

- **Systems responsive to feedback**—business systems that work like good closed-loop machine systems; that is, that adjust performance constantly and directly based upon feedback from the system's output to its input.

- **Fully integrated Dealer systems**—operating systems, business plans, and performance standards that are fully interactive.

- **Government policies that reflect the state of technology and don't add disproportionate cost** to the manufacture of product and/or research.

- **Dealer organization that consistently performs to standard.** Accurate forecasts, high CSi, profitable businesses, predicted inventory turns, highest possible sales efficiency, well trained retail employes, etc., are no longer nice to have. They are absolute musts.

- **A sense of teamwork on the part of Dealers.** Both players, manufacturer and Dealer, must see themselves as true business partners and act like it, particularly since product and customer service have achieved equal importance in the competitive mix.

- **Effective warranty management by the Dealers.** To ensure competitive cost-per-unit, GM must achieve parity (or better) in warranty cost management.

- **Consistent performance by Dealers and by contact people**—the bottom-line: doing things well, predictably, time-after-time.

- **A mass customization strategy** for products and services that will allow precise customer selection at a rate and cost comparable to mass production.

Deciding the 21st Century "Winner"

We have looked at today's automotive market, how it has changed from manufacturer to marketing-driven, and what the key strategies for future success are likely to be. Given all this, and the new alignment of European, Asian, and North American markets, what manufacturer is most likely to emerge as the big winner in the 21st Century? To project this, we'll call on industry analyst Maryann Keller's excellent new book *Collision*, and the author's own exhaustive analysis. To "cut to the chase," General Motors is definitely positioned to be the big winner, making the U.S. and NAFTA the leader in the coming century. The rationale for this conclusion is found in the following tables.

Toyota (Japan); Asian Consortium

- Strengths:
— Asian Market Potential
— History of Production Innovation
— High Quality
— Strong Customer Focus
— Developing Foreign Markets
— Huge Cash Surplus
— Worldwide Base.

- Weaknesses:
— Cultural, Economic Upheaval
— Reengineering (Secession)
— Productivity Offset by Strong Yen
— No Clear Vision; Share-to-Profit Shift
— Inflexible in Management
— Group Orientation
— Hard to Adapt
— Lack of Natural Resources.

VW (Germany)

- Strengths:
- — EEC Market Membership
- — Audi Resources
- — High Quality Reputation
- — Engineering.

- Weaknesses:
- — National Economic Conditions
- — Eastern Block Upheaval; Economic Weakness
- — Spain Operations Parts Network; Costs
- — No "Feel" for Voice-of-the-Customer
- — Marketing
- — Weakest in Productivity, Flexibility
- — Breakeven Point = Capacity
- — Entrenched Bureaucracy
- — Slow to Adapt
- — Not Customer Focused
- — Production System Farthest from Synchronous.

GM (America)

- Strengths:
- — High Quality
- — Best in Safety
- — Best Engines
- — Best Electronics
- — More Flexible (American Culture)
- — Strategic History of Market-Product Alignment
- — Non-Core Contributions
- — Involved in "Reengineering"
- — American Ability to Adapt.

- Weaknesses:
- — Product Strategy
     (Key: mid-size family sedan, minivan segments)
- — Capital Position
- — Non-core Costs
- — Vertical, Insular Culture
- — Cost-per-Unit.

- Key Factor:
- — Vision: Focus on the customer; Loyalty and Advocacy
- — Strategies to match the Customer-focused Vision.

While all three—Japan (Toyota), Germany (VW) and the U.S. (GM) have certain specific strengths and weaknesses, there are certain key points that stand out. Both Toyota and Volkswagen have some shared weaknesses that provide a genuine "window of opportunity" to General Motors and the U.S.

- The cultural and economic upheaval in both Japan and Germany has played havoc with costs, profits, and global market-share.

- Relative currency strengths have swung the price advantage to the dollar—for the present.

- Both Japanese and German automakers have been slow to adapt to the types of change that are counter to their cultural traits, i.e., cross-function team management that does not rely on "silo consensus" and the need to rapidly trim resources and expenses.

- Management succession changes are underway at both Toyota and VW.

- Government partnerships in economic planning, while productive during times of general economic and political stability, can prove cumbersome and damaging under political/economic pressure when a manufacturer needs to move fast and, sometimes, in a strategically "selfish" sense. For example, Toyota's need to leverage their immense capital "war-chest" and production resources to protect their global share strategy at a time when the MITI is pushing strongly for Toyota's support of other Japanese manufacturers.

The U.S., on the other hand, has some unique strengths that will allow them to take advantage of the opportunity window—**if** they act quickly and forcefully.

- The ability to respond and be flexible, as in answering the quality, safety, and customer-focus challenges.

- Technological innovation ability, particularly in engines and "underskin" electronics.

- Ability to align a full range of products to markets (cradle-to-grave) as part of a superior marketing strategy.

- And finally, the unique ability of the American culture to adapt and persevere under intense pressure.

In conclusion, General Motors and the American auto industry, due to traditional adaptability, flexibility and GM's refocusing on the customer as the core of its Vision, combined with its strong response to quality demands, will be the ultimate winner in the automotive business in the decade and the coming century. But the victory will not be a "given." It will require focus and implementation of the strategies outlined in this book.

There's no question that American ingenuity, flexibility, and the ability to create paradigm shifts in process, systems and technology innovation will position GM to win this leadership. As we've seen, a bit of "back to the future" thinking—updating Sloan's "car for every purse and purpose" (the cradle-to-grave strategy) must be revisited and updated to a "car **and customer services process** for every purse and purpose." General Motors and the American auto business did it in the 1920s. There's no reason to believe this team won't repeat and redefine leadership in the next century.

INDEX